Screaming in Silence

Suicide, Attempted Suicide and Self-Harm Recovery

Katy Sara Culling

chipmunkapublishing
the mental health publisher

All rights reserved, no part of this publication may be reproduced by any means, electronic, mechanical photocopying, documentary, film or in any other format without prior written permission of the publisher.

Published by

Chipmunkapublishing

PO Box 6872

Brentwood

Essex CM13 1ZT

United Kingdom

http://www.chipmunkapublishing.com

Copyright © Katy Sara Culling 2010

Chipmunkapublishing gratefully acknowledge the support of the Arts Council England.

For Declan; be at peace my love.
(Jumped in front of a train)

Screaming in Silence

INDEX

- Declaration
- Previous works by Katy Sara Culling
- Short Author Biography
- Acknowledgements
- General Introduction

Ch. 1. SUICIDE AND ATTEMPTED SUICIDE: *Absence can have great presence.*

❧Introduction.
❧Suicide: Life reduced to mere statistics.
  ♠ Figure 1: Map of latest suicide rate variation worldwide as recorded in March 2002.
❧Major Lifetime Risk Factors for suicide.
❧Further Discussion of Suicide Risk Factors.
❧Risk Factors for a suicide Crisis.
❧In a SUICIDE CRISIS, WHAT YOU SHOULD DO <u>NOW</u>:
❧Suicide Methods
❧More on suicide methods.
  ♦ JUMPING
  ♦ ASPHYXIA - HANGING AND SELF-STRANGULATION
  ♦ SELF-DROWNING
  ♦ SELF-CUTTING
  ♦ DRUGS! (LEGAL AND PRESCRIBED) CHEMICALS.
❧Doctors and Suicide.
❧The GREY-LINE between suicide and attempted suicide (and self-harm).
  ♠ Figure 2: The Spectrum of self-harm, through attempted suicide to suicide.
❧Suicide notes: the effect on the victim and those left behind.
❧Loss

♣Recovering from the suicide of an Adult Son by Tony Salvatore
❧Stigmatisation.
❧Treatments.
❧Religion.
❧Suicide and the Dangers of the Internet.
❧Suicide, Euthanasia and Assisted suicide.
❧Extinction.
❧HOPE.

Ch. 2. SELF-HARM: *Silent Agony.*

❧Introduction.
❧Why?
❧ List of Reasons why people self-harm. (Not fully inclusive).
❧Forms of self-harm.
❧The Risks.
❧Ways to help, and ways not to help.
❧The way you might get treated in hospital if you ask for help with a self-injury.
❧The basic NICE Guidelines for people who self-harm:
❧Dangers of the Internet.
❧ Survivor story 1: The Stepmother
❧Survivor story 2: The experience of self-harm without suicidal intent.
❧HOPE.

❧CONCLUSION

❧Recommended websites.
❧Recommended books and journals

Declaration

This is an anti-suicide, pro-recovery from suicidal ideation and pro-recovery from self-harm book. Whilst every effort has been made not to give out dangerous information that is not already freely out there, some of the subject matter is macabre and methods are discussed.

Screaming in Silence

Previous books by Katy Sara Culling

Dark Clouds Gather: The true story about surviving Mood disorders, Eating disorders, Attempted Suicide and Self-Harm.

Too Good For This World: True Stories from People with Mood Disorders.

Reflective Reflections: The Comprehensive Book on Eating Disorders.

The 'Gentle' Murders? (Fiction).

Screaming in Silence

Author Biography

Katy Sara Culling was born in Liverpool, North England, in January 1975, sharing her birth date rather aptly with Virginia Woolf. Daughter of Sue and Paul Culling, her family moved back to its roots in Derbyshire, where she grew up along with her younger sister Beth, in the village of Castle Donington, on the Derbyshire-Leicestershire border. However, even as young as 5 she exhibited symptoms of bipolar disorder (manic depression) – leading her to be loud and talkative, often in trouble. She also worried a great deal about death to an extent that is very unusual in one as young as she was. Not just her own death either.

She attended a private school for girls, Loughborough High School, where she was an extremely high achieving student. Unfortunately, due to bullying and also to numb her rampant mania and depression, she developed **anorexia nervosa** and began to **self-harm.** She found that the anorexia and self-harming took over her life and made coping with mood swings easier because she did not feel their full effect anymore.

Katy Sara then went to The University of Nottingham, where she studied Biochemistry and Nutrition. She did her (1st class) thesis on alcohol and metabolism, interested in the psychology of alcoholism. All this was done despite considerable illness including over 60 suicide attempts and purging-type anorexia – and yet more bullying. She was bullied for being anorexic by her fellow floor-mates. However her good academic work at Nottingham lead to an offer of a place at The University of Oxford, where she studied for a PhD (DPhil) in Clinical Medicine. Here she was a full time member of Linacre College Oxford and was never bullied.

Linacre is a graduate only college. She took part in many cycling events for charity.

In her final year she became so ill with anorexia and **bipolar depression** that she agreed to take time off her PhD (the worst decision of her life) and go into hospital (first as a day patient, then an inpatient on the general ward, and eventually a sectioned inpatient on the general ward). During those two years she attempted suicide over 300 times, dying twice, only to be revived. *She also made several trips to the Emergency Room to be treated for either suicide attempts or self-harm.* She finally, at the age of 28 got a diagnosis of **bipolar I disorder** and the correct medication, and had been mostly fine ever since. Her eating disorder spontaneously recovered when her bipolar disorder became more controlled. She later wrote up her PhD thesis and published her results.

Katy Sara now works for the Bipolar Foundation – Equilibrium, an independent, international, non-governmental organisation dedicated to improving treatment and understanding of the causes and effects of bipolar disorder ('manic-depression'). Katy Sara also works for Stephen Fry as an administrator and moderator of his website, focussing on *The Secret Life of the Manic Depressive* section, which is a supportive section of the forums for people who have mental illness or not. Obviously mainly people with bipolar disorder and depression write there and Katy Sara's personal experience is of great help. Katy Sara speaks publically at events about her experiences where many people feel ashamed to do so, her personal mantra being, "I do not hang my head in shame" (for being ill).

Now Katy Sara is mostly well and has become a writer, wanting to prevent others from suffering as she did. She writes mainly about bipolar disorder and anorexia but also other psychiatry/mental health topics, and her first book, her bipolar memoir ***Dark Clouds Gather*** (autobiographical) was published by Chipmunkapublishing.

Her second book, ***Too Good For This World***, a collection of stories from people with bipolar disorder and major depression is also available, including people with eating disorders. Katy Sara's third book, ***Reflective Reflections*** was a comprehensive but easy to understand book on all eating disorders – Katy Sara being a recovered anorectic herself. Both were published by Chipmunkapublishing – The mental health publisher. ***The 'Gentle' Murders?*** was her first book of fiction, also published by Chipmunkapublishing is not for the weak-hearted!

Katy Sara also spends her time working in medical research, and helping fellow survivors of anorexia, bulimia and bipolar disorder through charitable organisations whilst trying to maintain her own good mental health. She is an advocate for all survivors of these illnesses and believes that an "expert patient" system could be highly beneficial. She has not ruled out the possibility of doing another PhD, this time in Psychiatry.

Every day is a battle with illness that she wins, and she hopes that 443 suicide attempts will never reach 444 and so each day remains one that she feels she has won over her illness demons.

Katy Sara is a manic depressive, psychiatric scientist, academic, existentialist, comic, humanitarian, philanthropist, depressive nihilist, pragmatist, ambivalent, non-conformist, suicidologist, survivor, poet, editor and writer!

Screaming in Silence

Acknowledgements

Thank you to Mike Kerins, the artist who drew the front cover design known as 'Spike.'

For my three brave story writers for sharing so openly their experiences.

For my poets who wrote about their distress.

For my publisher for the 5th time.

For my family, always.

Screaming in Silence

General Introduction

> "The thought of suicide is a powerful solace: by means of it one gets through many a bad night"
>
> ❦ Friedrich Nietzsche (Philosopher, 1844-1900.)

A light-hearted start to a very serious pro-survival, pro-recovery book, written because I have been the survivor of many suicide attempts, not to forget also the person left behind after actual suicides, and the victim of serious self-harm in myself and those I love. What Nietzsche wrote is true, having a plan to hand can often help a person cope, but not harm themselves. I haven't attempted suicide or self-harmed for 8 years and I don't plan to do so again, but I always have my plan to hand.

Starting at the age of 11, I have attempted suicide 443 times (sometimes barely surviving, twice dying, only to be revived) and for fifteen years I was a person who self-harmed – cutting and bloodletting, sometimes as self-harm, sometimes as a suicide attempt. The two are definitely linked but not all self-harm is suicidal, not all suicide attempts are meant to kill, and sadly about one million people kill themselves every year, not all of them meaning to. As I have also been the victim left behind when someone I loved took their own life, I really can see the issue from all perspectives. Allow me to fill you in on my personal experience first of all, so you know you are 'talking' to someone who really has been there before herself. Pull up a chair, or sit back in bed, and we will talk.

Screaming in Silence

My suicide attempts, 443 of them, ridiculous you think! Obviously not very good at it you think! Probably didn't really want to die you think – wrong on the last one. In order to count something as a suicide, as we shall discuss in greater depth later, I had to have the full intention of killing myself, and think that I would kill myself, even though I failed. So when at the ages of 11 and 12 I tried to slit my wrists and took a whole box of ibuprofen I really thought, on each occasion, that it would kill me. My methods got more dangerous as my knowledge grew. I have taken over 300 overdoses of pills, only one time did this land me in hospital so ill they thought I'd die (no I'm not telling you what I took). I tried 60 times to gas myself to death with chloroform but obviously failed. The rest of my attempts come from cutting arteries, veins or more likely blood-letting using blood giving equipment stolen from the hospital I worked at as a clinical medicine PhD student. The two attempts that killed me were heroin overdoses, but on both occasions I was found and just resuscitated in time.

So, I know what it is like to attempt suicide. I know what it is like to be sitting there with a belly full of pills hoping it will kill you, or sitting there with a needle in your vein knowing that if you press the plunger you will end your life. I know what it is like to lie there for hours gradually filling up litre jugs with your own blood, and I know what it is like to realise all your efforts were futile. I know what it is like to believe your family will be better off with you dead, and how when you commit the act you are disconnected from those you love or you wouldn't be able to go through with it. I know what it is like to face your family after you survive a suicide attempt. It can be hard.

I also know what it is like to get the news or receive a phone call to tell you that a dearly loved partner has taken their life. In my case, the first time I collapsed to the floor, the second time I SCREAMED "Nooooooooooooooooooo" and threw the phone across the room smashing it. I know what it feels like to know that person is gone forever but in the worst way possible. I know how you feel you failed them somehow, and that if you had done something different maybe the outcome wouldn't be a suicide. I find myself unable to feel angry with the person but furious with the illness that killed them (bipolar disorder in both cases for me). I feel that as a person with the same illness and a great deal of experience in suicide, I should have seen it coming. I should have been able to stop it. I failed.

I also certainly know what it is like to self-harm. I started out as a young teenager scratching myself with a razor blade and by the end I was numbing my arm or leg up with local anaesthetic and cutting so deeply I always needed sutures – which I would self-administer if possible, or go to Accident and Emergency where I received some of the worst treatment ever. I stopped going to A&E after that and just treated my wounds the best I could with steri-strips and bandages. (It's impossible to suture your arm with only one hand, probably why I moved on to my legs, so I could self-treat). I also blood-let by inserting a blood giving set into a vein and just let the blood drain away. Not something I recommend – I did this both for self-harm and suicidal purposes. Different reasons on different occasions.

So yes, I've been there, done that, got the T-shirt, barely survived, and now want to help prevent others making similar mistakes or understand the question "why" in suicide, and maybe help YOU by writing this book.

Screaming in Silence

Ch. 1. SUICIDE AND ATTEMPTED SUICIDE: *Absence can have great presence.*

❧Introduction

> "To be, or not to be: that is the question:
> Whether 'tis nobler in the mind to suffer
> The slings and arrows of outrageous fortune,
> Or to take arms against a sea of troubles,
> And by opposing end them? To die: to sleep;
> No more; and, by a sleep to say we end
> The heartache and the thousand natural shocks
> That flesh is heir to, 'tis a consummation
> Devoutly to be wished."
>
> ❧ William Shakespeare (1564-1616).
> *Hamlet,* Act III, Scene 1, (written 1600-01).

Those are probably the most famous lines ever written about suicide and the contemplation of "self-murder," as it was known, during Shakespeare's lifetime. Until 1968, suicide in the UK was illegal! I will *not* be teaching you methods by which to end your days, although we shall discuss methods, there will be no step by step guide for how to kill yourself by anything which is not already covered and considered well known or easy to find information about out there. Instead I wish to try to relieve, empathise with the suicidal, show the potential suicide what their suicide truly means, and give some relief to those who have lost someone. I need to show everyone involved truths about the enigmatic state of being suicidal and the warning signs of impending, painful loss – of your own life or someone dear to you.

Derived from the Latin "sui" (self) and "cidium" (killing), the word "suicide" rather coldly describes the act of self-killing. It says nothing about the pain and torment that leads up to the terrible, final deed. I define suicide as *"an intentional, self-inflicted act that ends one's own life, the motives for which may or may not be known, but which seemed rational and purposeful to the victim, usually as a last resort, and often without any comprehension of the pain they would cause others."*

Attempted suicide is even harder to define, and will be considered in both this chapter about suicide and the next about self-harm. The simple definition would be that of *"an intentional, self-inflicted act that does not end one's own life, despite death being the main or only intent, for the same reasons that might be found in an actual suicide the motives which can be asked, and were enough to make suicide seem rational and purposeful to the victim, usually as a last resort, often without comprehension of the pain they would cause others."* At least with attempted suicide there is a chance to discover the reasons why – although these will always be extremely complex.

Suicide is not an act of weakness; devaluation of those who attempt or complete suicide does *not* help prevent suicide nor comfort those left behind. And such depreciation is rife; most people don't tell others if they have attempted suicide. Suicide takes bravery, pain, desperation, and usually the presence of a mental illness. A leading expert on suicide said that mental illness is "ubiquitous" in suicide – in other words, mental illness is always present. I would agree, except in some cases of euthanasia.

When depressed the person may not actually want to die, but feel forced to find an end the psychological pain they are in – and it just so happens that this results in death. For others death is a clearer, permanent aim, but still incidental to the absolute need for cessation of emotional and sometimes physical pain. Hopelessness can push *anybody* over the edge…

"Nine men in ten are would be suicides."

୭ Benjamin Franklin (1706-1790)

However suicide has long been looked at as the coward's way out:

> "To run away from trouble is a form of cowardice and, while it is true that the suicide braves death, he does it not for some noble object but to escape some ill."

୭ Aristotle - (384 BC-322 BC)

Absence can have great presence; think on that sentence. If YOU were to kill yourself, the feeling of your missing would be very much present in the lives of those who loved and liked you: so present it is almost tangible. Any loss can cause a hole in your heart that is forever with you. Never is loss deeper than in bereavement; and never more controversial, painful, angry, sad, and altogether devastating, than in the case of suicide. I know this personally. The experience of losing someone to suicide is, for some reason, more unrelenting than, and un-like any other loss in its destruction of both the victim and those left to pick up the pieces – sometimes quite literally. Certainly not better, not necessarily worse, but definitely very different in the depth and type of emotions stirred up: commonly anger, guilt, grief, shock, pain, puzzlement … and so on.

I feel these things every day: every moment that I remember every person I have lost to suicide. Their beauty as people destroyed, leaving a void that can never be filled. I am, however, a terrible hypocrite, as I am a person who is aware of all of this, and yet I have attempted suicide hundreds of times. I wanted to disappear altogether, and would have done so without hurting anyone, if I could.

Sometimes I still consider taking my life; sometimes suicide feels like the inevitable conclusion that awaits me: the exclamation mark at the end of a haphazard existence. I will not call it "a life." I have been, and might become, prepared to subject others to *my* absence: unable to see the pain I might cause, or think it "better" for everyone if I were gone. Knowledge that I could recover did not save me last time. I might again have faith that suicide is the answer to my pain, and a way to enable other people to at least cease fearing that I may eventually take that route. Once it is done, it is done: no more pain, and no more fear. Today I am aware that it is delusional to think people will be happier should I die. I do not always sense with such clarity.

In the suicidal mind, there is nothing but pain and desperation: lucidity is absent. A person's thinking is "paralyzed," they do not feel they have any other worthwhile options, and their mood is "despairing, and hopelessness permeates their entire mental domain."[1] In other words, suicide feels like it is a balanced, best and only solution.

I do not condemn suicide or attempted suicide; neither do I always think them to be irrational: I just don't think they are rational very often. None of my 443+ attempts had any lucidity; although at the time I would have defended their

---

[1] Professor Kay Redfield Jamison, (1999), *Night Falls Fast, Understanding Suicide*, Published by Alfred A Knopf, Inc., New York. p. 93.

logic to the death – literally. Sometimes suicide can be the best option, but only once all other options have been exhausted. The costs are always high; the end is always gruesome; there is no going back. Throughout history, people have chosen their time to die, and did not (cannot) feel regret in it. Had I died by my hand before this day, and were regretting possible in such an instance, I would be regretful.

Suicide is referred to as "a permanent solution to a temporary problem." In some cases you might liken it to visiting Madame Guillotine in order to cure a headache. But I am of two minds – I feel the deepest empathy towards those who wish to do with her or his own life what they will, even if that is to end it. I believe strongly in personal freedom, even if that autonomy is fatal. Yet I am still torn: I strongly desire to protect anyone I can from falling prey to suicide because I know life can get better. I want people to know that it is final. The end. No more life. No chance for recovery. I have been enticed by suicide's apparent promise of ending my heartache far, far too often, and I'm barely thirty-five. Like the genius Sylvia Plath, dying is an art I have practiced with passion almost all my life. Unlike Plath, I am still alive – today. And I am grateful for my life today.

Suicide is an accomplishment that is totally incomprehensible to many people, and yet perfectly logical to others (albeit often temporarily, and probably whilst insane – and there are those of us existential depressives who ponder death and suicide endlessly). Unfortunately, temporary "logic" can have permanent, very sad results. A suicide is something that fascinates people, and indeed, is a very final, vehement statement from the victim, be it an expression of anger, boredom, pain, a bid to say, "Fuck you!" to God, so on and so forth. I fear that many people feel they are finally expressing their feelings "poetically" in this way, when all that is left is misery, misunderstanding, and a corpse. There is nothing poetic about a cadaver.

I am fairly unusual to be able to write to you from the position of someone who has actually successfully committed suicide. However, medical science revived me to breathe some more. Many suicides, though by no means all, can be prevented. For now, I am concerned with helping you understand as well as is possible, the incomprehensible. I aim to explain the inexplicable, fathom the unfathomable, offer some hope, and create some closure.

ಱсултSuicide: Life reduced to mere statistics.[2]

Suicide is a primary worldwide health problem. The World Health Organization (WHO) estimates that one million people committed suicide in the year 2000, which is a horrifying number. Indeed in every country in the world, suicide is amongst the top three killers of people under the age of thirty-four. What is worse, as suicide is often hidden; we must assume that the actual figure is, in fact, much higher. These hidden suicides are particularly prevalent amongst young people who kill themselves, where a reluctance to admit the truth leads to verdicts such as "accidental" as the cause of death.

Suicide is a *major* public health issue in the UK, with just over 16 suicides per day, totalling 5,910 suicides *recorded* in 2001 (i.e. approximately 1% of the population). This is an increase on the 12 per day totalling 4,315 suicides recorded in 1995.[3] Note that for both given totals, there are approximately 2,000 additional "undetermined" deaths: an unknown number of these will have been suicide.

For every completed suicide, there are an estimated twenty to thirty attempts. Some never go reported; some cause serious injury; others need life-saving intervention. Of those people who attempt suicide once, 11% eventually succeed. In America there is also a terrible problem, with a person committing suicide every seventeen *minutes.* That is eighty-

---

[2] Detailed information can be found in the excellent suicide fact sheets provided by **MIND** (National Association for Mental Health). http://www.mind.org.uk/
[3] MHF *Briefing No.1 -Suicide and Deliberate Self-Harm, The Fundamental Facts*. (MentalHealthFoundation). http://www.mentalhealth.org.uk/

three lives lost a day or just over thirty thousand completed suicides a year.[4]

It is estimated that in the USA 300,000-600,000 people *survive* suicide attempts every year; 116,000 are hospitalized, 19,000 of whom are permanently disabled.[5] What I find astonishing is that in a country as advanced and health-conscious as the United States of America, the eighth leading cause of death, for *all* age groups, is suicide. As in the rest of the world, for people in the age group 15-34, suicide is the third leading cause of death.

♠ **Figure 1: Map of suicide rate variation worldwide as recorded in March 2002.**

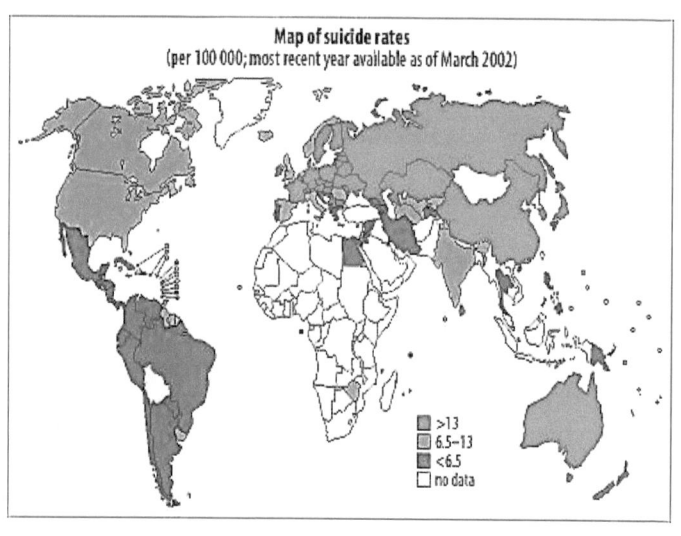

---

[4] Kochanek KD, Murphy SL, Anderson RN, Scott C. *Deaths: Final data for 2002. National vital statistics reports*; vol 53 no 5. Hyattsville, Maryland: National Center for Health Statistics. 2004.
[5] Stone Geo, *Suicide and Attempted Suicide: Methods and Consequences*. Chapter 1.

MAP REPRODUCED WITH THE PERMISSION OF
THE WORLD HEALTH ORGANISATION.

The previous diagram shows which areas of the world are most at risk. The UK, Spain and North America are both within the second highest band of suicide rates, where approximately 1% of the population die by suicide. Australia and most of the East and Russia are in the highest band. WHO figures on suicide that showed that recently the highest reported prevalence of suicides has been in Lithuania, The Russian Federation, and Belarus.

Although the suicide rate overall is slowly decreasing, several groups in society have an increasing risk, and have increasing suicide rates. It is towards these people that extra vigilance should be directed. Some people live with major lifetime risk factors, and, as such, it is these people that should be targeted for help to prevent the likelihood that they might slip.

Note that here we are discussing LIFETIME risks, ones that do not change or at least do not change rapidly with time. These factors are always present as a risk for suicide, it does not mean that the person is in crisis and needs immediate attention. For example, take the first risk factor – I have attempted suicide many times but I have not been hospitalised for eight years. Several of these risk factors are true for me, but I currently live quite normally.

❧Major Lifetime Risk Factors for Suicide.

Note that not all of these have to be present: *each is a considerable risk factor on its own*, whereas several risk factors multiply the lifetime risk. Risk factors are listed briefly as follows, with some further discussion afterwards:

❖ **Past History of attempted suicide.**
Between 20% and 50% of suicides have previously attempted suicide. People with previous "serious" suicide attempts are at a much higher risk for eventually succeeding. (By "serious" I mean with attempts with severe *intent* of killing oneself; the method itself can vary in potential lethality).

❖ **Psychiatric Disorders/Illnesses/practices**
Depression
Manic Depression/Bipolar I, and Bipolar II Affective Disorder.
Schizoaffective Disorder.
Schizophrenia.
Eating Disorders.
Self-Harm.
Alcohol misuse or abuse.
Drugs: substance abuse including street drugs and prescription drugs.
Personality Disorders.

These are all particularly problematic when two or several problems are present. I.e. a Dual or Multiple Diagnoses.

❖ **Access to lethal means.**
Doctors, pharmacists, veterinary surgeons and nurses have access to, and knowledge about, lethal drugs, as do some patients prescribed drugs that are potentially dangerous. Access to guns is particularly problematic in some countries and

professions. Police and those in the Army may have access to such weapons. Laboratory scientists have access to dangerous chemicals like cyanide or chloroform. Farmers can have access to dangerous chemicals and are likely to own a shotgun.

❖ **Impulsivity.**

Impulsive individuals are more apt to act on suicidal impulses. There are many lethal actions that require little planning, and a moment's impulse can terminate any possible future and resolution. Other people may patiently plan suicide, be ambivalent, and then often carry out the act in a moment of impulsivity. I always thought I was a very methodical, careful person, never a risk-taker, never out-of-control. Looking back, I see how wrong I was.

❖ **Sex.**

Males are three to five times more likely to commit suicide than females. Britain and America are alone in that they are the only countries that have diverging trends in male and female suicides. Between 1971 and 1998, the suicide rate for women in England and Wales almost halved, while in the same period the rate for men almost doubled[6]. Men are likely to complete suicide, more women are likely to attempt. What protects a female that might kill a male?

---

[6] Ibid.

❖   **Age.**
People, especially men, aged under thirty four and over sixty five are most at risk. The young and the old are the most at risk. Suicide is the third leading cause of death for those between the ages of 10 and 24. In America, figures show that whilst the elderly comprise only 12% of the population, they account for about 18% of suicides.[7]

❖   **Social isolation.**
This is a significant risk factor because not only do people living alone get depressed, but people who live alone have time and space to commit suicide without the risk of being found and rescued. It is noteworthy that practically every psychiatric illness carries with it an amount of social stigma, and/or social anxiety, further isolating the at-risk person, as in a vicious circle. Young or old; single, recently separated, divorced or widowed people are more likely to commit suicide.

❖   **Ethnicity.**
I have already illustrated how suicide risk varies depending on your home country. However, ethnic minorities within countries can be at greatly increased or decreased risk within what has become their home country.

---

[7] Ibid

❖ **Sexual orientation.**
According to research conducted in the past two decades, gay, lesbian, bisexual, transgendered and questioning/curious people have more suicidal ideation than their heterosexual peers. As such, they are at greater risk of attempting or completing suicide.

❖ **Genetic predisposition.**
There are no known genetic markers to predict psychiatric illness or suicide, however there is an apparent familial trait. Therefore if your family has a history of suicide, depression or other psychiatric illness, you should be more wary.

❖ **Detention in prison**
For a variety of reasons on this list, compounded by being locked up in demoralising and stressful conditions, it is not surprising that prisoners are at increased risk of attempted and actual suicide. A study[8] found that most prisoners suffered "multiple deprivations prior to their imprisonment." The rate of suicide within male prisoners is approximately 12 times that of the general population.[9]

---

[8] Liebling, A. Krarup, H., (1992), *Institute of Criminology*, Cambridge University.
[9] Summers, L. 2003, Reducing Self-Harm and Suicide in Prisons: Advice for Prison Staff on Using Safer Cells, Jill Dando Institute of Crime Science, University College London, found at http://www.jdi.ucl.ac.uk/downloads/crime_science_series/doc/SAFER_CELLS_NOV03.doc

❖ **Hopelessness about life and recovery.**
A general hopelessness is common, often leading to despondent plans for suicide. When the actual moment arrives where *all* hope is lost, this is when hopelessness becomes part of a suicide crisis as opposed to a suicide risk factor.

❧Further Discussion of Suicide Risk Factors.

If anything can be done to lower a person's risk factor for attempting suicide, it should obviously be done, such as seeking medication for a psychiatric illness, abstaining from alcohol and drugs, and counselling or therapy to learn of more positive ways to cope with emotional stress and anxiety. It is important to acknowledge or have acknowledged your physical and/or psychological/emotional pain – which often does not happen. Obviously there are many factors you cannot change, such as your genes, sex, age, race, sexual orientation, family history, or your previous suicide attempts. If these factors apply to you or someone you love, it is worth being extra cautious and aware of your situation should it begin to decline.

A Previous suicide attempt (or attempts) is one of the "best" indicators of future suicide completion. It is estimated of those whose suicide attempts are so serious as to need hospital treatment, 1% will kill themselves within a year, and up to 5% commit suicide within 10 years.[10] But take note that some people do not seek help even following drastic suicide attempts and so will be absent from these statistics. On

---

[10] Hawton, K. Fagg, J. (1998), *Suicide, and other causes of death, following attempted Suicide*, British Journal of Psychiatry, 152, p.359-366.

average, it takes a person who ultimately succeeds at suicide, *eight* attempts.

Mental illness is the leading cause of suicide and attempted suicide, bringing misery to the lives of millions, causing social isolation or even exclusion, thus worsening the risk of suicide. Ninety percent of suicides are thought or known to be the result of mental illness. Depression of any kind, including a depressive episode in people with bipolar disorder, is the leading cause of suicide, present in 70% of cases.[11] Of course social, psychological and physical stresses on the suicidal person will all be present. E.g. they may have lost their job, they may need therapy for PTSD[12], and their neurochemistry is causing their depressive episode.

People with mood disorders are between 5 and 15 times more likely to commit suicide than people without a psychiatric illness. As discussed, there are many types of depression, and the best way to avoid a suicide outcome is proper treatment as outlined in chapter 1. So if 70% of suicides are due to depression, does the type of depression increase or decrease the risk of actual suicide? In actual fact, *when* suicidal ideation is at its worst, when the person is most depressed, they are unlikely to have the energy to put together and implement a well-thought plan. (Unlikely: *not* never). Major depressive disorder/unipolar depression does not carry as high a risk of completed suicide as bipolar disorder. People with bipolar disorder/manic depression are at very high risk of completing suicide, 15%-17% higher than that of the general population.[13] Mixed episodes pose greater risk of suicide than

---

[11] Mental Health Foundation (1997), *Briefing No.1 - Suicide and Deliberate Self-Harm*, MHF.
[12] Post-Traumatic Stress Disorder
[13] Fuller Torey, E. *Surviving Schizophrenia. A Manual for Families, Consumers and Providers.* 4th Ed. HarperCollins. P 312.

either mania or depression alone.[14] When in a bipolar mixed episode the risk of suicide increases to 20%. Patients who are *psychotic* and have *severe* depressive symptoms *mixed* with mania are most at risk of harm or suicide.[15]

Schizophrenia, drug and alcohol abuse and eating disorders can also lead to suicide – probably because of associated depression and life events (such as being unemployed).

For example schizophrenics cannot cope well with the over-stimulation and chaos they feel in a social situation, especially if they are hallucinating or delusional – and, if they have insight into how ill they may become and what their illness costs them, they can give up, and take their life – this is a form of depression within schizophrenia that leads to 10% of schizophrenics committing suicide.[16]

People with eating disorders almost always experience depression that can lead them to feel suicidal and act on such impulses. Weight, food eaten/binged upon, having vomited, being unable to vomit, and exercise not done are all problems that can push a person with an eating disorder to drastic measures. Sufferers tend to hide away to eat; this can mean an anorectic's single yoghurt is stretched to last over an hour, or a bulimic's frantic, antisocial binge and vomiting session. Most of their life they feel out of control and depressed and speaking from personal experience I know these issues push you towards suicide.

---

[14] American Psychiatric Association. (2000) *Diagnostic and Statistical Manual of Mental Disorders.* 4th Ed. Text Revision. Washington, DC.

[15] Strakowski SM, McElroy SL, Keck PE, West SA. (1996) *Suicidality among patients with mixed and manic bipolar disorder.* Am J Psychiatry; 153:67 p 4-6.

[16] Fuller Torey, E, *Surviving Schizophrenia. A Manual for Families, Consumers and Providers.* 4th Ed. HarperCollins. P 312.

Self-harm is a worrying sign with regards to suicide; it will be discussed at length in the following chapter. Other mental illnesses that are linked to suicide are personality disorders. These are extremely complex problems to understand, and so only an expert's opinion should be taken.

Drugs and alcohol greatly increase the risk of suicide for two main reasons. Firstly, a person with a drug and/or alcohol problem is likely to have a more problematic life, including psychiatric illness. Secondly, when under the influence of drugs and/or alcohol, people make impulsive decisions to end their life, and some don't survive to regret it. Many suicide victims purposely assist their own death using alcohol, or sometimes drugs, to "help" themselves commit the fatal act. In 1999, the Department of Health (UK) reported that nearly 40% of suicides outside hospital involved alcohol abuse and just under 30% involved other drug abuse.

Looking at these figures from the opposite direction, general estimates are that approximately 15% of people with an alcohol problem commit suicide.[17] Men are more likely to have an alcohol problem, and when this happens they are 6 times more likely to commit suicide than someone in the general population. It is less likely for a woman to have an alcohol problem, but when she does; her risk of suicide is 20 times that of the general population.[18] Amongst people who abuse drugs, the risk of suicide is twenty times that of the general population.[19] Remember that a dual diagnosis of drug/alcohol abuse with another illness such as depression is very dangerous.

---

[17] Faulkner, A., (1997), *Briefing No.1 - Suicide and Deliberate Self-Harm*. Mental Health Foundation.
[18] Harris, C. Barraclough, B., (1997), *Suicide as an Outcome for Mental Disorders,* British Journal of Psychiatry 170, p. 205-228.
[19] Ibid

Sex matters. In the UK, covering all age groups, 75% of suicides are male, 25% female.[20] Suicide rates for men are higher than those for women across all age groups, although the gap between rates does vary. The most common cause of death for men aged between 15-44 is suicide, and has been since the 1980s.[21] Until recently males aged over 65 years of age had the highest suicide rate (24 per 100,000 population 1979),[22] but 2002 figures show that young men are starting to catch up reaching 22 suicides per 100,000). Fears remain that the incidence of suicide in young men will continue to increase. American men are four times more likely than women to be "successful" at completing suicide, despite some women now using guns. Men are more likely to succeed with a gun as they tend to shoot through their mouth or temple; women tend to shoot themselves in the chest, which has a lower mortality rate – though it's still pretty effective!

Women are more likely to *attempt* suicide (especially aged 15-19), but men are more likely to actually *complete* suicide. More women acknowledge that they suffer from depression – so why do fewer women die by their own hand? Just as in men (young or old), single, recently separated, divorced or widowed women are more likely to commit suicide. Generally women are protected from suicide because they are more likely to seek support, value their relationships to parents, partner and children more highly (I am generalising), and are more likely to seek out and accept psychiatric intervention.[23]

---

[20] Ibid
[21] Brook, A., Griffiths. C. (2003), *Trends in the mortality of young adults in England and Wales, 1961 to 2001*, Health Statistics Quarterly 19, ONS.
[22] Office for National Statistics 1998, Social trends 28, HMSO, London.
[23] American Foundation for Suicide Prevention 1997, *Suicide in Women*, in Suicide Facts.

These days, men are doing less well in their education and in terms of their career. Drug and alcohol abuse, particularly amongst men, is increasing. Marriage seems to protect men against committing suicide, and the rise in suicide rates may be partly due to the suicide increase in unmarried men.[24]

The fact that women are far more likely than men to attempt suicide, recently caused a woman at a mental health training course to ask me, "Are woman just crap at it or something?" The truth of the matter seems to be that not only are men less likely to seek help for distress, they are more likely to choose suicide methods that are *unequivocal.* Men choose more 'violent' ways to meet death. I am not saying men are necessarily more violent, just that jumping in front of a train and thus being slashed to pieces is somewhat more violent than taking an overdose. I supposed both are violent in actual fact, but the former is more likely to kill a person, do the job quickly, messily, and leave no time for intervention or a changed mind.

Age matters. For many years, the highest suicide rate could be found in adult males over the age of 65 (24 per 100,000 population in 1979).[25] Although this figure is not increasing, a large number of men die by their own hand due to mental and physical illness, physical pain, isolation, guilt and hopelessness. Many older people who kill themselves received little or no help from professionals. The only good news is that the suicide rate amongst the elderly in the UK has consistently decreased over the past fifteen years. In America, the overall suicide rate is still increasing with no decrease in the suicide rate amongst the elderly.

---

[24] Charlton, J. et al. (1992), *Trends in Suicide Deaths in England and Wales* Population Trends No.69, Office for National Statistics, HMSO.
[25] Office for National Statistics 1998, *Social trends 28*, HMSO, London.

In *one third* of the world (mainly in Western, developed countries), for the first time, the suicide rate amongst the young is now overtaking the suicide rate in the elderly. Peer pressure, mental illness, exam stress and an increase in the availability of drugs and alcohol mean that in the UK, 19,000 young people (under 15-24) attempt suicide every year, 700 of whom die as a result. Horrifyingly, every 30 seconds, a UK adolescent (age 10-19) will attempt suicide, eleven percent of whom will be successful then or on further attempts within two years.

Suicide is the second leading cause of death for people aged 15-24, accounting for 20% of all deaths.[26] In terms of the actual number of deaths, it is for men aged 15-24 that the suicide rate has risen the most over the last two decades: From 9 per 100,000 in 1979, to 13 per 100,000 in 1999 – a rise of almost 50%. Figures have also gone up for men between 35-44 and women between 25-34. The greatest percentile increase (of 75%[27]) of has actually been for women, aged 75 and over, shown in 2002.[28]

Social isolation is both a cause of despair and a risk factor, as it allows suicide to be completed without discovery. Most suicides take place *alone*. If you move home and find that you live alone it is worth the effort to create a social network, keep in touch with family and old friends – even getting yourself a dog or cat is helpful. If you are a student (anywhere) feeling isolated, there will be help provided by your College or University if you seek it out. Anxiety is also a common factor that can lead to isolation in people who are at

---

[26] Samaritans 1998, *Exploring the Taboo*, The Samaritans. Website: www.samaritans.org

[27] Note that the increase of 75% does NOT mean 75% of elderly ladies kill themselves; it is a comparison of the *rate* of Suicide in the past and present, the actual rates are low.

[28] Samaritans, 2004, Information resource pack 2004, Available: www.samaritans.org/know/pdf/InfoResourcePack2004web.pdf

risk. Many people with psychiatric disorders also suffer from general-anxiety and social-anxiety.

Ethnic minorities within countries can be at increased or decreased risk within what has become their home country. African English and African Americans, living in a predominantly white society, particularly young black men, are at a much greater risk than their white counterparts. Asian women (age 16-24) have a suicide three times that of 16-24 year old women of white British origin. This is particularly alarming since male Asians have a suicide rate that is below average. Thus maybe strict family values, religion, and being expected to undergo arranged marriages may all contribute.[29] Problems for ethnic minorities that contribute towards mental illness and suicide are racism, discrimination, violence and poverty. Complex cultural barriers exist, as do language barriers. Ethnic minorities are less likely to receive the correct treatment, and metabolise medication differently, meaning the correct needed dose is higher or lower. Atypical symptoms are often presented. More research is needed in this area. American Indians and Alaska natives have a suicide rate 50% above average, whilst Hispanics have a lower suicide rate than average.

Sexual orientation can be a huge risk factor. According to research, gay, lesbian, bisexual, transgendered and questioning/curious people have more risk of suicide than their heterosexual peers.[30] Quoting from a Department of Health leaflet, those at increased risk of suicide include people "whose sexual orientation brings them into conflict with their family or others." Many experience parental

---

[29] Raleigh, V.S., Balarajan, R.. (1992), *Suicide and Self-Burning among Indians and West Indians in England and Wales*, British Journal of Psychiatry, 129, p.365-368.

[30] Bridget, J. (1994), *Treatment of Lesbians with Alcohol Problems in Alcohol services in North-West England*, Lesbian Information Service.

disrespect, even losing their home whilst relatively young, together with violence, abuse and misunderstanding that may continue throughout their lifetime. It is not possible to change your sexuality to "rectify" your problems. Some people become isolated and/or turn to substance abuse which may in turn cause a psychiatric illness – all are risk factors for suicide.

Actual suicide attempts are thirty to forty percent more frequent than in heterosexuals. This is particularly problematic in young people, and/or ethnic minority people who are also gay. A report commissioned by the US Government in 1989 concluded that gay and lesbian young people were 2 or 3 times more likely to attempt suicide than their peers, and that they may account for 30% of youth suicides.[31] Sexual orientation is not recorded on death certificates. The good news is that alternative sexual orientations have become more acceptable as people become better educated and therefore less prejudicial. More research is needed in this area.

Hope is so vital, and when it is lacking life feels so grey. Knowledge and understanding of illness can lead to *despair*, especially if illness returns and the victim feels it cannot be endured once again. Because of insight, and because of the likelihood of knowing what is lethal, *education* can increase the risk of completing suicide, with suicide being the second leading cause of death for American college students.[32] (Note that lack of knowledge can also mean something that is not meant to kill, does kill).

It is my belief and experience that the worst risk factor for suicide is hopelessness, which can be a short-term crisis risk,

---

[31] Lesley, T., (1993) *Victims of a Moral Crusade.* Pink Paper, 9th March.
[32] Ibid

or a long-term risk factor, or both. It is the short-term absolute hopelessness that can push people over the edge. People exist with many debilitating mental problems, and live with them for a long time, sometimes for years; but when hope is lost it can be the "last straw." If – or rather when – the sufferer loses all hope, it can mean death.

But what can you do to help? Can suicide be prevented? The truthful answer is no, not *all* suicides can be prevented, but many can. Even when someone is plummeting towards death with intelligence, knowledge, lethal means, and all the energy they can muster, their suicide can be prevented, as I am testimony to. I cannot lay out a list of stages a person will go through that takes them from normal to the point of taking their life – there are far too many variables and it is different in each instance. Some of my experiences are laid out later in this book to show you what made me reach crisis point – sometimes it took very little.

While some suicides occur without any outward warning, that is not typical. People are afraid to talk or ask about suicide for fear it might trigger a person to actually do it. This is not true, and many people welcome the relief to talk about what has been weighing heavily upon them. Many people, 75%, visit their doctor not long prior to the event, a significant proportion within the week prior to their suicide. Doctors should be aware (and some are) of the risk of depression, and that people who are suicidal might present with symptoms not associated with suicide. They might give themselves away by admitting or showing signs of a suicide crisis. (See later suicide crisis list).

The most effective way to prevent suicide among loved ones is to learn how to recognize the signs of someone at risk, take those signs seriously and know how to respond to them. *Always take a threat of suicide seriously*. People might set their affairs in order, write a will or suicide note. You can spot signs of the emotional crises that usually precede suicide, talk to the person and get help if you are at all doubtful that the suicide attempt is beyond your power to prevent.

The build-up of signs that someone is in immediate danger, signalling a time period where they are actively suicidal, is termed a "suicide crisis." This means they are in immediate danger of taking their own life. Note that a suicide "crisis" is different to a suicide "risk." Suicide risks are the long-term risk factors (already listed) such as concurrent psychiatric illnesses, age and sex etc. People can live a long time with suicide risks, even high suicide risk. But when a suicide crisis occurs, drastic action needs to be taken to prevent them acting on their suicidal impulses.

The signs of suicide crisis must then be considered along with the person's suicide risk, based on their medical history, age, sex, past attempts at suicide and psychiatric disorders. *This assessment needs to be done by professionals*, and might result in hospitalisation, either voluntary or involuntary. Sometimes hospitalisation is only for a few days or a couple of weeks. Indeed nowadays it is usual for such admissions to be short, though there are unfortunately exceptions.

❧Risk Factors for a Suicide Crisis.

Eighty percent of people who plan to commit suicide give signs of their intended action. These signs (*not all have to be present; indeed one is quite enough*) you can recognise. As you can now see, suicide is not as rare or inexplicable as people imagine, and it is a serious problem, particularly if you remember that for every completed suicide there are a number of people left behind to grieve this unfathomable loss, which will be covered momentarily. For now, the warning signs to look out for in yourself or someone you care for if you are in a suicide crisis necessitating professional help for yourself or a loved one, are:

❖ **Precipitating Event.**
Almost any recent life event that is upsetting to you/the person involved. (If you are protecting someone else, keep in mind that something you don't consider important or 'bad' might feel catastrophic to them). Common examples include bereavement, possibly even a friend's suicide, events such as the breakup of a marriage or relationship, being diagnosed with a terminal illness, or loss of a career, bullying, doing badly at school or university exams, being raped or attacked, or not getting into the university of choice. Or it might be suddenly realising that you/they are ruthlessly trapped in an illness, such as anorexia that has been ongoing without your full awareness, or suddenly deciding that you/they will never recover from something like depression.

❖ **Intense moods in addition to Depression.**
Usually people who commit suicide do it with *desperation*. This might include desperation to resolve a situation such as on-going illness where death represents closure. Also common are one or more of the following: *torment*, *guilt* (e.g. for hurting people left behind), *anxiety*, *anger*, a sense of abandonment and above all, <u>*hopelessness*</u> that anything positive can happen ever again.

❖ **Changes in emotional behaviour.**
Intense moods may be present, but do they change? A colleague, friend, loved one, or you yourself, may begin acting in ways that seem unusual. Someone usually content suddenly being sad and withdrawn. The classic example to be wary of is a person who has been depressed, maybe for a long while, suddenly cheering up and being happy. They won't tell you that this is because they have made the decision to end their life and hence suffering, giving them some sense of peace. (You may also be able to notice these happening to you if you are suicidal).

❖ **Any spoken or written communication suggesting the person might soon commit suicide.**
Many people give clues about what they are thinking of doing, perhaps with the last remains of hope that someone might help, or in order to say goodbye to people, even asking for unconscious permission. They

might say something like "I might not be around." Some people say things quite obvious but sometimes it is more discreet, such as saying that other people would be relieved if they were to die, but not actually saying that they will die or are planning to die. Some people write a suicide note, or similar and leave it where is might be found. These might even be on the computer.

❖ **Definitive Actions.**
Writing a will, giving away special, treasured items, buying a gun, buying drugs, and/or buying lots of alcohol. Effectively putting one's affairs in order, purchasing items with which to commit suicide and/or things to help them manage to kill themselves such as alcohol or drugs.

❖ **Self-destructive behaviour and decline.**
A decline in personal behaviour and in level of functioning. This can be at home, socially orat work. You/the person might get angry, upset, drink more, use recreational drugs, overuse prescription drugs and/or behave strangely. Note that such self-destructive behaviour might actually cause a *precipitating event* such as loss of a driving license for driving whilst drunk, or losing a job due to reduced capability, thus adding to the suicide crisis.

❖ **Recovering from Depression.**
When people are very depressed they often do not have the energy to put together and

carry out a realistic, lethal suicide plan. When you/they have begun to feel a little better, you/they feel slightly more energetic but still depressed. This extra energy can cause you/them to put their suicide plan in to action. I assume this is applicable to psychiatric disorders other than depression, but concurrent depression is highly likely in these.

❖ Release from psychiatric hospital.

Many suicides take place shortly after a person has left the relative safety of a psychiatric ward. This is because the person may be pretending to feel better to get out and commit suicide. Or they may have more energy due to partial recovery (see reason above), or actually they cannot cope with their life when released, particularly if hospitalised for a long time. At this time family or friends are vital and should be aware of this risk and does anything appropriate to prevent it. Checking or even watching whilst medication is being taken (particularly if it is dangerous in overdose) is a good example. That tip saved my life.

Inpatient suicides account for up to 16% of deaths, which may seem like a large number of people, until you consider that many of the most at-risk people will be found in a psychiatric hospital population. Psychiatric wards are often busy, understaffed, and some people "slip through the net" in this way, when checks that should be made are not or people manage to escape. Escape from many psychiatric wards is not difficult if one is determined.

Many suicides occur when patients are allowed leave from the ward, be that for an hour or much longer. The time people are most at risk, and when most suicides take place, is when they have just recently been discharged from psychiatric in-patient care; 24% of deaths are found in people who had been discharged in the previous three months. In most cases, as you might expect, medical staff believed the person to be at low risk. In some instances (like for myself), patients are released despite being high risk; this is because they are not benefiting from, or being kept safe by, hospitalisation.

❖ **Reckless behaviour, "Russian roulette type behaviour."**
Driving dangerously, wasting or giving away money, not caring about things that were once important to you/the person. Even up to playing Russian roulette or behaviour you could liken to playing Russian roulette such as reckless abandonment, cycling like a mad woman in and out of cars and buses in Oxford. This behaviour can include a lack of concern for the future, such as taking up smoking despite understanding the associated risks, because you/that person feels that they have no future to worry about.

❖ **Self-harm.**
Additional self-harm, (cutting, burning, overdoses, etc.) which might be of escalating frequency and/or severity with respect to how dangerous and life threatening it becomes.

❖ **Return of psychiatric symptoms after a period of recovery.**
Veterans of psychiatric illness will recognise the return of an illness that they consider too awful and painful to experience again. I *cannot* return to depression, and were it to happen again…

❖ **Physical illness, particularly if painful and or terminal.**

When you or someone you love is in a suicide crisis, here is what you should do immediately.

❧In a SUICIDE CRISIS, WHAT YOU SHOULD DO NOW:

1. Call for assistance where you live and seriously consider ringing 999 (UK) /911 (USA) straight away.

2. Do not leave the suicidal person alone, or be alone if you are suicidal.

3. Trust your instincts, follow these procedures listed below, as it is better to get help and be safe than to leave it and regret it for years or end up dead.

4. Talk to them about your concerns and *listen*. Do not be afraid to ask questions. This will not "put ideas into their head," or make the person become suicidal if they are not already.

5. Do not be judgemental. For example, do not say, "How could you want to kill yourself and upset me so much?" The suicidal person will probably feel guilty about this already, and will certainly feel too bad to cope with judgemental comments. They will be highly emotive, but not rational, and may overreact. You will be emotional; that is natural; but you have to be the strong one, and think before you speak.

6. Do not promise confidence about what they tell you because if you need to seek outside help, breaking this promise will spoil your relationship, and might mean that on a future

suicide crisis, the person is not honest with you.

7. Determine if the person has a specific plan to carry out the suicide. The more detailed the plan, the greater the risk. For example, do they plan to use a gun; have they already purchased a gun; is it loaded and ready; is it nearby? Does the person plan to overdose; have they bought alcohol to help them; have they decided what to use; have they purchased or saved up pills they want to use? Are the pills already popped out of the container ready to swallow? Have they already overdosed?

8. If you can do it without leaving the person alone, remove any means of attempting suicide that you can think of such as guns, knives, drugs or medications. Certainly remove any dangerous items the person has with them.

9. It is better that the suicidal person does not drive, especially not alone.

10. Do not try to counsel the person yourself: if you recognise these signs, you must get professional help.

11. Take them to their general practitioner for an emergency appointment, call 999 (UK) or (911) US or a psychiatric hospital to be assessed, or even an emergency department of a hospital if you are suitably alarmed. It is better to assume the worst and

act accordingly, than have a dead friend or relative.

12. Be proactive. The person you care about might be deliberately unhelpful to the professionals trying to help. Explain your concerns to the doctors, and offer evidence, especially of a suicide plan if you have it.

13. If the suicidal person resists all help, get it anyway. If you cannot make them go with you to get themselves help, speak to the professionals yourself, and if necessary the person can be assessed at home or brought by force to be assessed. Then they might be sectioned (hospitalised involuntarily) for their own safety, or hopefully persuaded to go into hospital voluntarily.

❧Methods.

People are always fascinated by the methods others use to execute themselves. It is a morbid fascination that I do not understand, yet am also drawn to. It seems to make the method of death more important and more memorable than the individual victim. I cannot criticise this fixation, for it is something I have always been guilty of obsessing about. However, I am determined that this book is *not* one that will focus too closely on the question of "how" to kill yourself. We all know ways to kill ourselves; and we all think we know ways to kill ourselves that are remarkably unlikely to work – assumptions that I am not going to correct.

There is a wealth of information available to help people end their lives. There are books; there are doctors; there are people and organisations that will help within and against the law in various countries around the world; plus a million methodological options to choose from in various situations. People cut, stab, poison (overdosing on street, prescription and non-prescription drugs), drown, jump from heights, jump before trains and traffic, crash vehicles, immolate, shoot, hang, strangle, smother and gas themselves. Each person's choice is individual, but most have a lot of thinking (however disordered) behind it. The "reasoning" behind a chosen method is in fact far more interesting than the method itself.

Common factors are:

- ❖ **Time**.
  How long it will you be in pain, how long until consciousness is lost, before being disabled, and of course, until death.

- ❖ **Pain.**

People often want to minimise pain – although some choose painful methods if they are quick – others prefer a less painful option that take longer. Again, a lot of people have miscomprehensions and end up alive, some disabled, suffering much more than they thought they would, or die when they really meant to use a suicidal gesture as a cry for help.

❖ **Reliability or Effectiveness.**
Some methods have a higher chance of death. Shooting yourself in the head or jumping in front of a train both have higher probabilities of death than an overdose or slit wrists. However, people survive shooting themselves in the head... and people die from overdoses. No method is 100% reliable or 100% safe. A lot of people would rather choose a more dignified and personal form of death than being hit by a train – I should know, I lost one partner that way.Reliable.

❖ **Determination**.
Not quite the same as reliability, it is the person's resolve by which they choose and use a method: some methods are far more likely to be lethal, although there is a lot of misinformation and misunderstanding. Determination may change during a suicidal act, should the chosen method be one that allows time for regret. Any method(s) is (are) lethal if undertaken with enough fortitude. (Indeed a person may choose one method, and then add a second or more in order to speed up or increase the certainty of success). Determination to die has *conscious* and *unconscious* components that may be in agreement or direct opposition.(Hence sometimes giving the appearance of

ambivalence). For example a determined person may cut deeper than someone more ambivalent, or someone more determined may get angry that their overdose is taking a long time to act and also cut their wrist or throat.

❖ Chance of Intervention.

Many people who intend to die will injure themselves when alone and within a time frame that minimises the chance of them being discovered and "saved." Sometime a person's situation means they will attempt suicide in desperation even though there is a chance of them being found – for example on a psychiatric ward.

❖ Consequences of failure.

Many people are aware enough to consider the possibility of failure and either choose some method with a low risk of surviving, or one that has less chance of leaving them disabled if they live. Of course, since all suicide attempts are potentially lethal, all have the risk of disability if rescued (e.g. paralysis due to brain damage). Other consequences include unwanted hospitalisation and having to deal with the anger/upset of loved ones.

❖ Risk to mental health of others.

People are usually aware on some level that their death will upset those that care for them (even if there is the misapprehension that this short, sharp shock of death is better for all involved). Hence this means people choose ways to be found by people other than their family, or methods that seem more humane. (Of course, discovering a body is fairly devastating on anybody, even professionals who "should be used to it.") Some people do not choose methods that they think will disturb even strangers – such as not jumping before a train because of the train driver, or not jumping from a height for people to see. Some people choose to just disappear, although I have been made aware that most families would rather know if their loved one was alive or dead.

❖ **Risk to physical health of others.**

If a method is such that it might injure or kill another, it may be avoided. For example crashing a car may be avoided in case other vehicles are involved. Jumping in front of vehicles may be avoided as this might cause an accident that harms other people. Most suicides would be horrified at the thought of taking another person's life. (An exception to this would be a suicide pact whereby both parties agree that they want to die. Being in a suicide pact increases the risk of suicide). Recently a suicide pact was made over the internet by two strangers one from the USA one from the UK who met up and committed suicide together.

❖ **Unwillingness to "contaminate" home.**

Some people choose to kill themselves away from their home, particularly if it is a shared home with relatives/friends. People go to hotels, kill themselves in their car, or in other places so as not to leave the memory of their death in their home. This also reduces the chance of discovery and being saved. (However, a large number of children and adolescents who kill themselves do so at home, with parents in the home).

❖ **Cadaver appearance.**

Many people do not want their dead body to look unpleasant – either for their own peace of mind, to protect the person finding their body, or the relative identifying it. Therefore some gruesome methods are not chosen. Having seen in person or in pictures the real life truth of a suicide's dead body; it puts me off. People should look at cadaver pictures on the internet so that they know what they will be leaving – it put me off many times. There is nothing poetic or beautiful about death.

Firearms are now the most likely choice of method in our American cousins, both male and female. On several occasions I had considered getting on a plane, just so I could shoot myself. The second amendment means Americans believe they have the right to keep and bear arms. I believe that preserving the individual *right* to bear arms is different from the *actuality of carrying guns* around so freely. I do not wish to get into politics, particularly those of a country I do not live in: but in my personal opinion, it is simple common sense that guns should not be so easily available anywhere. They are designed for one purpose: to kill. I am extremely glad that guns are very hard to get hold of here in England, for it is apparent that even allowing for the difference in population size, Americans are killing themselves faster than we are, and I am sure. If I could have procured a gun at any point I would have no doubt used it.

As mentioned, the question of where to commit suicide is almost as important as the question of how. There are hot spots for suicide, such as Beachy Head on the south coast in England. It takes six seconds before you hit the rocks (so I hear). I know the Golden Gate Bridge is a favourite – they've even brought out a film of real live jumpers. It's not a fool proof method however, people survive.

On one of my many visits to America, at the tender age of 19 in New York, I went up the Empire State Building. The first thing I noticed was the barrier to prevent people jumping to their deaths. It annoyed me, even though I could never jump! Far too messy, and I might hit someone else, and … so high. I feel sad that my visit to a fantastic city is marred by such memories, but I have to accept that this is how my mind works. I am guilty of an excessive number of suicide attempts, but I know I am not the only person who has been absolutely determined and failed. I have died and been brought back. I have a dear friend who put a gun in his mouth and kept pulling the trigger but nothing happened. From my time in hospital I know many people who have taken things right up to the wire, determined to die, but somehow saved…

"Tired of life, Ms Elvita Adams decided in
1979 to jump
off the 86th floor of the Empire State
Building. She said,
"Goodbye cruel world," and leaped,
whereupon a
sudden, freak gust of wind blew her back
through an
open window on the 85th floor, where she
found herself
alive."

❧More detail in methods

OK, to get right down to it we have to discuss the main methods. Most of these you will already know about and I will be writing to you from the prospective of say a concerned lecturer, not wanting to put ideas into your head whilst discussing the topic freely, thoroughly and hopefully having put you off the idea for good. I will not be going into detail about any method rather than to tell people the negative effects of each type of choice. This book is anti-suicide.

♦ JUMPING

Many survivors claim to realise they have made a mistaken the instant they let go. As for the rest who knows because this is a reliable method for suicide if the drop is far enough, i.e. over 150 feet. I could never do it. I cannot contemplate those slow seconds as you fall and wait to smack into the surface. There is a risk of hurting someone else if you land on them, and there is a great risk of ending up alive and a quadriplegic, totally reliant on others, depressed and unable to do a thing about it. Only 2-3% of suicides come from jumping. Diving head first is most reliable but I spent time on a psychiatric ward with a man who tried that but rotated in mid-air and crushed his legs.

♦ ASPHYXIA - HANGING AND SELF-STRANGULATION

If you want to hang yourself properly you can easily find the drop distance (how far you need to fall through to break your neck rather than just hang there and choke to death) on the internet so I don't think it is added risk to discuss it here. Plenty of school children have found it online to tragic consequence. The formula used is:

$$\text{Drop in feet} = \frac{1260}{\text{Weight in pounds}}.$$

That's if you want your neck to break – and it is *not at all reliable*. You may just choke slowly to death, or you may rip your head clean off – mmm lovely. And of course there is the problem of finding something that will take your weight, getting the knot position right, tying the right knot, having the correct tense in the rope…and more issues I am not going to give a glimmer of an answer to here. Just letting you know it is by no means simple.

I have a friend who discovered her partner's body hanging and it destroys her to this day. The cadaver that is left is not pleasant to look upon, the head tending to be purple due to trapped blood. It is a method that suggests the person is serious and has a high mortality rate at 80%.[33] There is of course the possibility of brain damage if interrupted and saved at the wrong moment.

For self-strangulation, since the victim would pass out, a ligature is needed that will keep the ligature/rope tight so that air doesn't re-enter the victim preventing death. Suffocation, about which I am sad to say I know of a real-life case, comes from covering the head with for example a plastic bag and then not allowing air to enter the bag again. In the case I knew of the victim sealed a plastic bag at her neck with masking tape.

A more modern version of this is to have a can of nitrogen or helium blowing into the head bag so the person still feels like they are breathing, but of course they are getting no oxygen and soon die.[34] There is less distress because the suicide feels like they are breathing but they are getting no oxygen – this is supposed to lead to them feeling high, then passing out, then death.

---

[33] Suicide and Attempted Suicide by Geo Stone p322.
[34] Forgive I am not giving this website link I believe it too dangerous. The determined will find it.

The use of cyanide is asphyxiation at a cellular level. Anyone using hydrogen cyanide will die and certainly is not ambiguous about their decision to end their life. Not a nice way to go though. Fortunately few people have access to it. Using carbon monoxide poisoning from a car would be another such example of suffocation at the cellular level by the removal of enough oxygen carrying capacity of red blood cells when they instead bind to carbon monoxide which they have a high affinity for. Of course most cars have catalytic convertors and so using cars for the source of the carbon monoxide in newer cars is slow.

♦ SELF-DROWNING

On 28 March 1941, Virginia Woolf (a victim of bipolar disorder) put on her overcoat, filled its pockets with stones, and walked into the River Ouse near her home and drowned herself. Woolf's body was not found until 18 April 1941 where it was found by a group of children playing.[35]

Self-drowning is not an easy way to go but it is a determined way to go. It has a high mortality rate with approximately 80% of those trying it dying from it.[36] There is a potential for brain and lung damage if rescued but it requires no expertise or planning, the person can just do it.

However, it is important to note that drowning is nothing like it is shown on TV, i.e. not so fast. The drowning person may be conscious and inhaling water and extremely uncomfortable for up to 7 minutes in fresh water and 5 minutes in salt water (which also stings like a bitch). It's not

---

[35]Panken, Shirley (1987). ""Oh that our human pain could here have ending" — Between the Acts". Virginia Woolf and the "Lust of Creation": a Psychoanalytic Exploration. SUNY Press. pp. 260–262.
[36] Suicide and Attempted Suicide by Geo Stone p 207.

just a case of inhaling a couple of breaths of water; you have to keep on doing it.

If I were to come across someone who had tried to commit suicide this way I would consider them highly suicidal. Mostly men choose this method.

♦ SELF-CUTTING

Cutting appears to be the most 'safe' option as statistically it is the least lethal, with only 5%[37] of suicides that try to die by cutting succeed - however, it does work, and deciding whether it will work often depends on where the person decides to cut. A cut throat is fast, reliable and rather unpleasant for the person finding them – lots of blood and a badly maimed throat area. It requires a will of iron to perform – I know, I've tried and only been able to make small cuts – and I was desperate. Other areas the blood loss will be much slower, and as I learned, despite a lot of blood loss, are not always fatal. Other cons are that it is painful, and you leave the possibility of a permanent scar if you live, a gory cadaver if you die. Blood loss is always shocking in real life and nothing like on TV.

Pros include that razors and knives are easy to get hold of. You are unlikely to harm anyone else by your chosen method and you don't lose consciousness immediately giving you chance to change your mind. Or you can barely scratch the surface... cutting can be as serious a cry for help possible or as serious attempt at suicide as you make it, which is why there is such a misunderstanding about self-harm and attempted suicide.

---

[37] Suicide and Attempted Suicide by Geo Stone p.185

♦ DRUGS! (LEGAL AND PRESCRIBED) CHEMICALS.

The fatality rate varies hugely depending on what drug is taken – 1.2% to 11.4%, though this is still low compared to many of the methods we have looked at. Many drugs take hours to become toxic which is good if you want to back out, some are irreversible – a big disadvantage if you change your mind. Many drugs and poisons are actually quite painful and if they don't kill leave permanent damage. As I have found out many times, there is no such thing as a guaranteed lethal dose – I have taken 4 to 50 times the lethal dose of various drugs and survived. I have heard of people who have died taking just 7 paracetamol – under the recommended daily dose and well below the usual fatal dose which I'm not telling you. Overdoses are unpredictable. It is also important to note that if using the drugs just to self-harm, **there is no such thing as a safe overdose** either. One problem with drugs is that it is easy to act on impulse and many people end up taking their prescribed psychotropic medication as their overdose. Prescribed drugs are obviously dangerous in overdose. How dangerous depends on the particular drug. All overdoses should be treated as potentially lethal and the very least you should do is ring *NHS* direct or go to the Emergency Room.

Some people swallow bleach or other household items, these can lead to burning of the oesophagus (food pipe) and medical attention needs to be found immediately – the same is true of and similar household poisons. Take the bottle of what you have swallowed with you to hospital.

Street drugs can be very lethal, even when not cut with rat poison or baby laxative it's easy to overdose because the strength can vary so greatly, as can your believed tolerance. Take cocaine – it can cause a heart arrhythmia and kill you but there is no way to control it. Heroin on the other hand, an overdose of heroin injected into anyone would be lethal without medical treatment – I know, I tried to kill myself that way but someone raised the alarm and saved my life, twice. But I meant it. I meant it 100%.

❧Doctors and suicide.[38]

Doctors are the professional group most likely to kill themselves, particularly psychiatrists. (Possibly because people like me get drawn to that particular branch of medicine). Doctors have knowledge about anatomy and pharmacology, as well as access to lethal means, and the ways in which they choose to exit the world are therefore interesting in itself, and to compare with the general public. Doctors reading this book are at more risk than any other group – based on the possibility of copying my behaviour.

My doctor partner who committed suicide 5 years ago could not have done without easy access to the medicines used allowing them to steal insulin that was later overdosed on. Proof to me in real life that doctors are as fallible as the rest of us. I know other doctors who do not work or struggle to work because of illness.

Doctors have an elevated suicide risk and this has been suggested to be due to their access to lethal drugs. Keith Hawton *et al* found that between 1979 and 1995, UK doctors were far more likely to use self-poisoning than the general public (approx. 57% in doctors vs. 27% in the general public) Barbiturates were the most frequent drugs used, and certainly what I would have used if I had access to them.

The only medical speciality findings were that anaesthetists tended to use anaesthetic agents they had access to (as would

---

[38]Hawton, K., Clements, A., Simkin, S., Malmberg, A., (2000) Centre for Suicide Research, Department of Psychiatry, University of Oxford, Oxford, UK *Doctors who kill themselves: a study of the methods used for Suicide.* Oxford Journals QJM: *An International Journal of Medicine* Volume 93, No. 6 p. 351-357.

I have done), and psychiatrists that self-poisoned did *not* use psychotropic drugs to which they would have access, probably because they knew that death is unlikely to occur following an overdose of these drugs.

Self-cutting and piercing was also more frequently used as a method of suicide compared to the general public, possibly because doctors know where to cut to best cause death. I wonder if the doctors anaesthetised themselves prior to cutting, as I did, or if their piercing was the same as some of my attempts – directly into a vein with a large needle to cause blood loss.

Fewer doctors compared to the general public drowned or were found hanged, and fewer jumped from a height.

As I am only too aware, female doctors are twice as likely as other women to kill themselves: 13.6 per 100,000 compared with a rate of 6.3 per 100,000 for the female population as a whole. Interestingly male doctors have a lower suicide rate than other men. Maybe male doctors are more aware of treatments available to help them therefore come forward for help or self-prescribe. The rate for male doctors was 14.3 compared with a rate of 21.0 per 100,000 for other men.

❧ The GREY-LINE between suicide and attempted suicide (&self-harm).

> My thoughts went as follows: *I'm feeling depressed and scared, there's no point in living, I'm obviously not worth saving, no one thinks I am ill, ... so I'll kill myself.* I just could not see a way of returning to my old life: imprisoned in Linacre College, with all the death, self-harm, thoughts, emotional pain, endless nights, blood, needles, scalpels, suicide attempts, boredom, overdoses; with an ominous hallucination of a threatening Dark-Man-over-my-shoulder for constant company, a picture on my wall that talked to me, and a computer that floated above my desk. It *never* occurred to me to just say any of this to someone."
>
> ❧ Katy Sara Culling, *Dark Clouds Gather.*

During that time in my life I was regularly self-harming and sometimes attempting suicide – there was a difference, quite clear in my head, which it was. Mostly here we are concerned with the attempted suicide that so nearly became suicide.

The grey line between suicide and attempted suicide is a very fine line. On one side is oh-so-final death, on the other, some form of existence: treatments are needed, and there are a million possibilities for the future. There are many causes behind attempted suicide: a "cry for help," where there is no aim for death, a true determination for suicide completion (death), a desire for temporary peace, a need to end pain ... the list goes on. Approximately 140,000 people attempt suicide each year in England and Wales alone.[39] Of these, 1 in 5 will try again, of whom 10 per cent will succeed.[40] That's a lot of dead people many of whom could be helped.

It's often suggested that survived suicidal gestures are "attention seeking," implying time wasting - but I would dispute that, or otherwise say, "so what?" This is an unhelpful form of stigma attached to the desperate action some people are *forced* to take. I prefer the term "cry for help." A cry for help is a valid and serious cause of suicide and attempted suicide – not someone wasting time. However, it is generally frowned upon, leading people to hate themselves even more, and, possibly, commit suicide.

Many attempted suicides are serious attempts at ending life, and as such, cannot possibly be classed as attention seeking. I think we need to redefine what we mean by using the term "attention seeking." Attention seeking is not a heinous act: it is a symptom, and absolutely necessary in people who use it. I happen to believe that even if half-hearted suicide attempts are attention seeking, then that person *damn* well needs help and attention. If they were not desperate then they would not resort to such dangerous methods. There are many much better ways to get attention if you need it, without risking your life. Some people "crying for help" do unwittingly kill themselves when they do not know, or underestimate how dangerous their behaviour is. People think that they will pop "x" number of paracetamol tablets and be fine, and then they die. Attempted suicide for whatever reason is *dangerous*.

There is a spectrum of suicide, intentional attempts at death, and self-harm (which will be considered in the next chapter). Often the true reasons are only known to the victim.

---

[39] Samaritans (1998), *Exploring the Taboo*, Samaritans.
[40] O'Shea, B. *et al.* (1986), Aspects of Deliberate Self-Harm, British Journal of Hospital Medicine, 35, 5, p. 335-337.

♠ Figure 2: The Spectrum of self-harm, through attempted suicide to suicide.

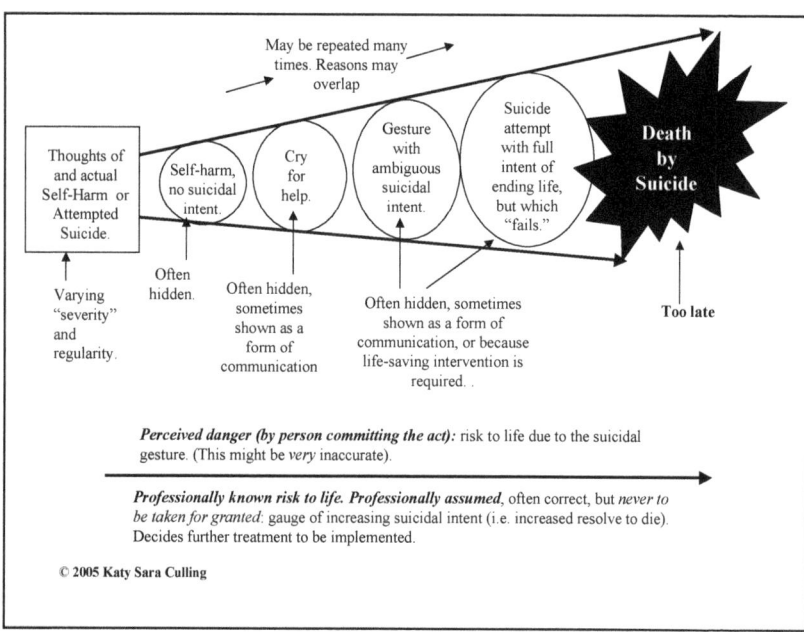

Note that at ANY point on this spectrum a person may die, be wrongly assigned, or have their situation change rapidly. No position on this spectrum is seen as more important, deserving, or more valid than any other. Two or more positions may be taken up concurrently. What can certainly be true is that suicidal people circle between many states of mind, perhaps understanding the pain they will cause when planning suicide. They put together a plan, but can still be ambivalent about the actual act. They then might impulsively use the prepared means of self-destruction during a time when their thinking is clouded.

Following attempted suicide by any method: what defines a "serious" attempt whereby a person must be kept safe? When should friends, family, or professionals intervene? The answer is that this is a very difficult problem to assess. Is it based on the medical lethality of a chosen method? This certainly gives some indication of how serious a person is to take their life. I think it can tell us that that person was serious, but we cannot assume that apparently less dangerous attempts do not have the same serious intentions. Speaking to the patient, if possible, is vital.

There is a huge difference in the short-term treatment needed for someone who was unwillingly brought back to life and expresses the wish to die, to someone presenting and the Emergency Department (ER) with a small cut denying any suicidal ideation. But both may be as determined to die. Both require assistance; both may get less that they need. Psychiatric services in the UK are so stretched that it is often only the most serious cases that there is room to treat… Eventually that girl with a small cut could end up dead or far more ill, needing long-term intensive treatment that could have been avoided had better treatment been available earlier. All forms of suicide and attempted suicide involve, by definition, at least one act of self-harm.

On any of the occasions I attempted suicide, I would have been determinedly annoyed if I had been told I had "just" self-harmed. Don't get me wrong, I have self-harmed, I know it is extremely serious too, but I did it for different reasons. (See next chapter). I would have been equally angry at the reverse misinterpretation. I was also often annoyed by the nonchalant attitude towards my self-harm or attempted suicide (those few times I was caught). I was never taken seriously. Never referred on to psych services, with one exception where I nearly died, and then they just spoke to me, I lied through my teeth and was let go. The reason behind any act of potentially suicidal self-harm is vitally important in determining the treatment and immediate risk to that person and their treatment.

Unfortunately, people lie: family, friends, and professionals can only do so much. *This means your life is ultimately in your own hands.* I have lied about my suicidal intent, claiming it to be absent. I have questioned and supported people who I knew to be suicidal, *only to have them lie to my face that they would be OK* and they have gone on to attempt or complete suicide. Believe me, at times I took a lot of convincing. But if someone is determined, they will take or try to take their life. However, that is no reason to give up trying to help them. And it is no reason to blame yourself if the worst does happen, although that is easier said than done.

❧Suicide notes: the effect on the victim and those left behind.

"To my friends: My work is done. Why wait?"

❧ Inventor George Eastman, committed suicide March 14, 1932.

You may be surprised to hear that a suicide note does *not* accompany most suicides; only one third of suicide victims leave behind some form of a suicide note. Some leave massive letters, some a few lines, and some write poems. Some people quote other writers or leave some form of communication (like email, a recording, or a book left open at a certain page). Some leave a list of requests or things to do.

Why do so few leave a note? I am sure that some who do leave a note do so because it is expected. However, many suicides are impulsive, leaving no time for a note. Some have nothing to say, or cannot find the words. I spent hours composing my suicide notes, but could never say all that I needed to say. I never left a note – not ever, although I wrote many. I found that writing a note made me think of those I loved, and as such I could not go through with the deed. Thus I stopped writing.

Suicide notes can help those left behind find closure and achieve a greater understanding of an immeasurably painful situation. However, some suicide notes can be unhelpful, if they are angry, or if they become an unhealthy and constant reminder of how that person died.

Here are some examples of suicide notes.

> *"I do love you all and I hope you know that there is nothing any of you could have done to change the outcome. Goodbye, with love."*

> ❧Suicide note of Katy Sara Culling aged 15 (never used).

Hopefully a note like this would alleviate guilt and provide some peace of mind. It illustrates the importance of hope for the future of those left behind.

Below is a note left following clear case of suicide in terminal illness to advocate for the right to die with dignity (i.e. via suicide or self-euthanasia); when the author was suffering from terminal cancer she chose to drink chloroform instead. This too provides closure.

> *"When all usefulness is over, when one is assured of an unavoidable and imminent death, it is the simplest of human rights to choose a quick and easy death in place of a slow and horrible one."*

> ❧ Charlotte Perkins Gilman, writer, died August 17, 1935.

Virginia Woolf wrote 2 suicide notes (that we know of), both to her husband (not one to her sister as sometimes depicted). One she wrote 10 days prior to her actual suicide on around Tuesday 18th March 1941 when she attempted to drown herself and then returned home soaking wet claiming to have fallen. The second she wrote before her "successful" suicide on March 28, 1941. Both letters are incredibly caring towards her husband, showing her distress at the thought of hurting him, yet contradicting herself with comments about him being better off without her, feeling certain that she is going mad again and fears she won't recover again. She repeatedly tells her husband how good he has been to her and that no two people could have been happier together. As already mentioned Virginia Woolf then drowned herself by weighing herself down with stones, leaving her walking stick, and walking into the river Ouse in Sussex, England. In 1949, only eight years after her death, lithium was found to be successful in treating bipolar disorder…

A suicide note in the form of a poem, as shown below, was left to the ex-lover who had just broken up with the suicide victim.

When I am dead, and over me bright April
Shakes out her rain drenched hair,
Though you should lean above me broken hearted,
I shall not care.
For I shall have peace.
As leafy trees are peaceful
When rain bends down the bough.
And I shall be more silent and cold hearted
Than you are now.

ತ Poet Sara Teasdale, suicide in 1933.

This is an example of where the note could result in a mixed response from those left behind, assigning blame for her death to someone else, alleviating guilt from others, but not giving a "good" reason for ending of life. The anger is quietly palpable, albeit understandable and terribly sad.

❧Loss

> "She always told me that if she did it (again) it would take her one attempt: and she was right. I saw her fly high for a wonderful week. And then crash into a dark depression through which nobody could penetrate – and I know I tried my best. I spoke to her for many hours on the night she died. I asked if she was at risk, if she had any suicidal plans or anything dangerous with her. She replied convincingly that she had no plans and nothing with which to harm herself with. Unfortunately I believed her.

I will never forgive myself for that…"

❧Katy Sara Culling, *Too Good For This World.*

Never did I contemplate suicide without immense self-torture about the pain I might cause. The suicidal acts themselves were carried out whilst numb, unconnected, unthinking, in pain, and in desperation. None were done whilst my wits were intact. Instead, I was *unable to connect emotionally in any way to those I love.* I existed in a world of pain that had to cease; nobody else lived in this world, so there was no one who would be hurt – at least, that is how it felt.

It may help you to know that a lost one did not leave the world aware that they would cause you such pain. A few angry suicides do intend to hurt people, but these are in the minority, and probably aggravated by mental illness. Suicide is unlikely to succeed if a person were not so ill as to *not* feel love, *not* be able to connect, not be able to comprehend, or remember that they loved you so much. Many suicides labour under the misapprehension that people would be happier were they not alive – Virginia Woolf being an example of this, writing in her suicide note to her husband about wasting his life and that he'd be much better without her.

A suicide victim's pain (I/we assume) ends with death, and it is at that point where for everyone else, the pain boils over into an uncontrollable mess of thinking: *could I have helped, if only, I'll miss her/him, ouch, what more could I have done, why, why, why?* And emotional overload with anger, disbelief, pain. Suicide deeply, painfully and horrifically affects everyone around them. Parents lose a child; children lose a parent; people lose a sister or brother, a friend, a lover, a patient, a colleague. Whoever is lost to suicide leaves behind pain and questions that cannot ever be satisfied. I imagine (I do not know) that it must be the kind of pain worst for loving parents who bury a child, although it is fairly shit for all involved. Remember how the number of young people taking and trying to take their own life is on the increase.

Nobody should have to bury their own child. I know that I cannot begin to describe what it is like to lose a child to suicide, so I asked a friend who bravely agreed to help me understand. He agreed to write about how he is coping with his loss now, but asked me to introduce some facts to you first. Tony Salvatore lost his son to suicide in November 1996. To try and combat suicide, he has bravely turned his life around to working to help prevent suicide and I highly recommend a visit to his website should you find yourself in this unfortunate position. (See back of book for reference).

We call a child who has lost its parents an orphan. What is the word for a parent who loses a child? There isn't one. Because it's too awful to consider?

Now we turn to real life. When Paul committed suicide, Tony, his father said he was left torn between three main emotions: loss, anger and pain, and "lots of each." He described it as the "eternal triangle of parental grief," that he could not escape from. Tony felt that his son's suicide left him incomplete. Saying that it, "tore something out of me and I will never be the same again." He described the loss he felt like a black hole, like he had a hole inside where he had lost his precious son. He said, "I'm not whole and the hole won't close. All loss is shit, suicide loss is the worst shit. Losing a kid to suicide is off the frigging shit scale."

Once the shock wore off, the anger came: anger that his son Paul did not need to die. Anger that some people could have prevented it, some even knew of Paul's pain and plan but did nothing. Tony also feels angry with himself, feeling responsible and angry for missing Paul's suffering. Eight years on, his anger remains unchanged and as intense.

Finally, there is the pain, piercing right into Tony, getting worse when "the inescapable reality of what happened sinks in." Then it becomes a chronic pain, omnipresent. It still hurts, but then in a different way. "There are times when it still gets very bad. It's always there. It's something that I live with. Something that I don't need." At the time, Tony wrote:

> The Parents Left Behind
> Forever mourning the lost child;
> Forever lamenting the lost dream;
> Forever facing the hole in the future;
> Forever feeling the hurt in the heart;
> Forever reliving the unbearable horror;
> Forever regretting the act not done;

Forever searching for the reason;
Forever seeking release for the love.

☙By Tony Salvatore.
In Memory of Paul A. Salvatore, (1968-1996).

That was how Tony felt closer to Paul's death. Since Paul's death in 1996, Tony has drawn on his loss in order to help others at risk of suicide or those coming to terms with a suicide of a loved one. Here is a letter he hopes will help similarly at-loss parents reading this, and maybe even help prevent suicide in some cases.

♣ Recovering from the suicide of an Adult Son

> On November 13, 1996, I lost my oldest son, Paul, to suicide at the age of just 28. At that time and for about two years afterwards, I never thought that my life would ever again be something that I could describe as "normal."
>
> The loss of a child to suicide intensifies the emotions that come with losing a child by any means. It also amplifies the intractable psychological turmoil brought about by any suicide. With the suicide of a child of any age it seems to be even more so for the parents. I see no need to revisit those feelings here. *I would like to try to recount how I believe that I came to get past them over the years.*

As I write this I am living what has been called a "new normal life." There are very few moments in the day when Paul is not in my thoughts. However, while my loss is always with me, my grief does not dominate my life.

I am a different person. I am not better or stronger, just different. I am more acutely aware of my vulnerability. I have many more anxious moments in regard to my wife, my children, and my grandson, than I feel that I would have if we had not lost Paul.

At times the enormity of my loss makes its presence felt. There are moments when I miss Paul so much that I am immobilized. A memory, a picture, something that I associate with him may trigger one of these moments. Writing this has done so.

These moments are frequent, but fleeting. They pass, as do the tears and the brief shudder of pain that washes over me. I can handle these episodes because I see them as the price of a love that will only end when my life is over. I will never let Paul go.

Still, I can characterize myself as having recovered from Paul's suicide. I never had a conscious goal of doing this. Basically, I just wanted to survive his loss. I was able to do that and more. That's what I want to share with you.

They say that everyone grieves differently and I am sure that we each have our own path to recovering from grief. As I look back on what I think helped me, I will try to focus on the aspects of my experience that others might relate to rather than what is unique to me.

My recovery began about two months after Paul's death when I attended Survivors of Suicide support group. The facilitator had also lost an adult son. She had come to terms with her loss and she said that her pain had given way to a sense of regret. I didn't believe that I could ever get to where she was. My grief was very acute. However, I now felt that it was not endless, or ever growing.

While I strongly advocate that any suicide griever participate in a suicide loss support group, I only did so for a few meetings. That was enough for me to learn that my family and I were sadly far from alone in our bereavement. Understanding that we were not alone and that what we felt was normal, helped greatly.

The Internet proved to be a powerful coping resource. Like many who lose someone to suicide, I didn't know enough about suicide to deal with the questions pulsing through my mind. I knew a little of suicide from a sociological perspective, but this was of little value. I read almost everything that I could find on suicide. Within a few months I had constructed a very simple causal model of sorts in my mind. It did not provide closure, but it countered the myths and misconceptions that assailed us from all sources.

On the Internet I ran across mail lists for suicide grievers and web sites memorializing lost loved ones. I joined a list and it was a means of mutual self-help and support. I was helping myself by helping others, and this aided my progression towards recovery.

About a year or so after Paul died I decided to do a website in his memory. I opted for a format where I could share what I was learning about suicide and suicide loss. The content was guided by the questions that I tried to answer for others. One page became several and building them soon became my principal self-help strategy for the next three years. This work made me feel very close to Paul.

The pages put me in contact with people all over the world. I heard from the bereaved, but also from those who were or who had been suicidal, and from those interested in suicide prevention and grief support. Except for the grievers, most of those I heard from didn't want to know about my loss. This compelled me to become conversant about suicide on a different level.

I dropped off the mail lists as the pages took more of my time. I was "doing something" but I didn't feel that I was doing enough. Next I had a few articles on suicide prevention published. This involved documenting what I had to say, and pushed me further towards a depersonalized understanding of suicide. I now had an implicit grasp of how my son came to die and that was sufficient. I did not need to know what specifically happened.

I also had a wonderful personal experience that had an overwhelming effect on my recovery that continues – *I became a grandfather*. In 1998 on the day before Paul's birthday my daughter gave birth to a little boy. Immediately a troublesome time of the year became less so and here was someone whose helplessness transcended our own. And his middle name is Paul.

Our grandson has in no way replaced our son. Rather he has made it much harder to be unhappy and centred on our loss. At the time that he came into our lives we didn't really care a lot about living. We weren't suicidal but we simply had little motivation to live. As we were involved in his care we had to start caring a little more about ourselves.

My grandson put some sense of the future back. However, *the loss of a child is the loss of an envisioned future, the loss of a long nurtured dream.* There's always a void out in front of you, and, at least for me, it makes it very difficult to care about long-term outcomes.

Getting back to my self-help strategy, these days my energies have turned to more local interests. I am on the board of the Survivors of Suicide (SOS) group in my area. I helped to start suicide prevention task forces in two counties. I am on the staff of an emergency psychiatric hospital that has a suicide hotline and other crisis intervention services.

My job and my volunteer activities obviously sustain my on-going recovery. I am deeply involved in my employer's suicide prevention efforts. Suicide, suicide prevention, and suicide loss are things that I deal with every day. I do what I do for Paul and for me.

I think that sometime after losing Paul I decided to move in this direction at some level. I gradually shed my former career (or maybe it shed me) as well as friends who had trouble with my "preoccupation" with suicide.

So here I am, such as I am. I guess I could be better, but I am better than I once ever thought that I would be. What I did worked for me. Others can put together a recovery strategy that fits their lives. Hopefully some of what I have shared will be of use.

Tony Salvatore[41]
Springfield, PA (USA)

As you can see from Tony, suicide inevitably leaves behind a multitude of agonising emotions and misunderstanding: anger, hurt, loss, and pain, almost beyond bearing, and lasting for many years after. This has also been my experience. And yet I understand the Suicidal impulse. I know I could do it again. I've crossed that line so many times that it is altogether too "easy."

I have known many people admit with undeserved guilt, that they are actually relieved that their loved one's suffering has ended. After a long drawn out illness or illnesses, (mental and/or physical) death can result in release for sufferer and their loved ones. People who admit to this feeling are often very ashamed, but I think it is eminently understandable. It is also noteworthy that whilst some people do feel this sense of relief, they are still distressed and hurt tremendously by losing someone they loved.

---

[41] SOS: Survivors of Suicide Website: http://lifegard.tripod.com/

❧Stigmatisation.

"Once it is over, your life is over, gone, forever, blackout, nothing, oblivion. There is no coming back, no chance of regret. You can't feel or regret anything when you are dead. At least, I fucking hope so."

❧ Katy Culling, age 27, diary.

When someone commits suicide, either they disappear quietly into oblivion, or there is some warped circus, which analyses all the "facts" and a thousand different opinions are formed. Occasionally a suicide is a glamorised news item, or a gossip-worthy event, or far worse, a blaming session; but because of fear of the stigmatisation, most suicides are hidden, or if not exactly hidden, information is not publicly offered and discussed. People don't tend to share personal information about suicide.

At the coroner inquests, not only a verdict of suicide is recorded but also "accidental," "misadventure" or "murder," even, "normal" causes are recorded. So many suicides go unnoticed on a societal level, though never on a personal level. Emergency and medical staff will know of course, but in confidence; and the coroner will also know or suspect. The family might know, and the friends might suspect. Sometimes, even facing incontrovertible evidence, the family will not believe a suicide verdict. Generally, no one shouts about the facts, and the perceived "shameful" explanation for reason of death is not shared.

Stigma concerns the attempted suicide survivor, it concerns the family and friends of those who attempted or died. There are support groups out there (see recommendations). The only person the stigma no longer concerns is the "successful" suicide victim because they are dead.

People have strong opinions about suicide, and many jump in with damning condemnation about how selfish it is. Few suicides are particularly selfish; all are deemed as such. We could debate the semantics of the word "selfish," but let's not. Much in life is selfish without it being bad. True: suicide is a selfish in that it inescapably devastates those people left behind in a way no other death can. However in this selfishness is *unavoidable* and *unwanted.* In almost all suicides, this selfishness is something that torments every victim, and stays their self-execution until the pain of life has become *so* unbearable: life is "simply" not an option. Unless you have felt this extreme agony, you are not qualified to blame anyone for her or his decision in such circumstances. If you have truly felt this misery, you will already know that blame is neither helpful nor applicable. It is not about hurting others; it is about finding a way through an impossible pathway.

Trust me: suicide usually takes a lot of commitment and nerve, not cowardice. When you slash at your throat, you instinctively move backwards. People are robust; they don't die nearly so quickly or easily as you may think. I am a testimony to that fact; as despite serious, lifelong commitment to end my life, I am miraculously still here. Not many people would survive through my experiences and live to tell the tale. But that is all I did: survive.

❧Treatments.

You cannot "treat" suicide: once it is done, it is too late. Suicide must be *prevented*. Suicide and attempted suicide are caused by other problems rather than being a diagnosis in their own right, although a person can be described as "suicidal" or as having "suicidal ideation."

In order to prevent suicide, the reasons (usually mental illness) behind the desire to kill one's self need to be addressed, usually with medication, psychotherapy or counselling, and help with social circumstances. Treatment for suicidal crises involves keeping the suicidal person safe until the immediate risk has diminished in the best way possible. Usually this means admission to a psychiatric hospital where means of danger and freedom of movement are removed. Such crisis treatment is not intended for long-term management of suicidal ideation; general psychiatric wards are not exactly therapeutic places conducive to improved mood.

Outpatient crisis intervention teams help to manage people at risk of suicide at home by providing support. Regular contact with your General Practitioner, Psychiatrist and a Psychiatric Nurse and Social Worker if you have these, are all helpful ways to keep you safer and out of hospital. Hospital should be a last resort, but never shied away from if the risk is too high. People at high risk should be watched one-on-one in hospital or by loved ones – all of whom must resist manipulation. Therapeutic communities are also a possibility for people with long-term mental health problems including suicidal ideation. I have seen them work wonders.

❧Religion.

> "No green leaves in that forest, only black;
> no branches straight and smooth, but knotted, gnarled;
> no fruits were there, but briars bearing poison."

❧Dante's Inferno, Canto XIII.
Where the poet and Virgil enter a forest
where the trees are the souls of suicides.

As an atheist, I assumed it would be easier to commit suicide than if I were religious and believed it to be a sin, and thus I would go to hell. I have since learned that was an oversimplification: religion is not necessarily protective against suicide; it can be, but people can rationalise a way to reconcile suicide and their beliefs. Doubts creep in about any belief system, even atheism. Rose Langridge, a friend who believes strongly in God, but who suffers from chronic depression and anorexia, and who has attempted suicide five times, shares below how she was able to reconcile this with her faith:

> *"Although in the eyes of the church suicide is wrong, I convinced myself that God wanted me to die ... he was showing me a way to be happy and free again. I drew a picture that shows the contrast between my life on earth and the relief I would find in Heaven. In the picture God is saying, "Come to me" and smiling. It made me feel so much better when I thought about dying and going to him. My mum says it wasn't God who put the idea in my*

*head, it was the Devil but I'm not sure. On
bad days I still long for death."*

I had a friend who committed suicide despite devout Catholicism, in fact, just after a visit from her priest. I have learned that Atheism does not make suicide easier. Nothing makes suicide easy.

❧Suicide and the Dangers of the Internet.

"Welcome to ***; sorry you're here."

❧ Traditional welcome page greeting on a popular suicide website

The information available on the Internet is either extremely helpful/informative, or tremendously dangerous and liable to lead to disability or death, depending on who you are and how "lucky" a person is when following the instructions they find. There are instructions, as mentioned, telling you what length of rope to use to hang yourself (so that you do not choke slowly, or accidentally rip your head off). There is even a *time-agony-lethality* calculator, that compares how methods vary in the time it takes to die, how much it hurts, and how likely it is to result in death. In other words, if you are suicidal, or know of someone who is, the Internet is a dangerous place.

I believe in freedom of information, but if an at-risk friend, relative, colleague, or child of mine were looking at such sites, I would find ways to stop them. There is a large amount of incorrect, misinformed "advice" that could lead to a slow, painful death, or worse, survival combined with a significantly lowered quality of life. One lady I know has ended up paralysed from the waist down after she attempted suicide with a small drugs overdose mixed with gin.

Do not expect that posting a suicide note on any website will bring intervention that saves your life. It might, it might not. (See also the *self-harm Dangers of the Internet* on this topic). Also, do not post that you intend to commit suicide and then be angry if someone does intervene – it happens all the time.

I don't want to give you examples of advice given from these sites that you may follow so am going to plump for the ridiculous! An example of website advice that I doubt will inspire someone to copy it:

> *"Decapitation is a technique that may induce rapid unconsciousness. The handling and restraint required to perform this technique may be distressful... Data suggest that electrical activity in the brain persists for 13-14 seconds following decapitation. ...Decapitation may be aesthetically displeasing."* [You don't say].

These suicide websites are (I think, but I am not sure) well meant, intending to help those wishing to end their lives with dignity, but caution is advised. Death is never dignified. I must reiterate strongly that there are a lot of medical errors recommending actions that could cause you severe pain and permanent damage. There is some advice I "laugh" at in the sense that it is very unlikely to be fatal, although it will be messy. There is also a lot of accurate, potentially lethal advice.

These sites inevitably encourage suicide, provide contacts for suicide pacts, suggest how to get hold of dangerous items, and give recipes for death: they are exceedingly dangerous for vulnerable people of any age, with any illness or problem. Some of these websites may actually strengthen the urge to end your life, and become a focus of unhealthy attention. (They did for me). Only recently, (late 2010), a couple met on the Internet, set a suicide pact, then by some chemical reaction (it was never reported what) died together in a car filled with this gas. People are far more likely to commit suicide in a pact than if alone.

Since getting hold of cyanide is hard for most people, I will include this example of advice asked on one of the website forms:

> *Advice seeker: "Hi, what happens if I drink alcohol before drinking my cyanide solution?"*
>
> *Website advice: "In the case of cyanide poisoning, I do not think that a small amount of alcohol would make much difference to the outcome..."* [Honest I suppose].

These sites are dangerous and if you are suicidal or can control the access of someone to these sites do not trust them or stop the sites being used at all.

❧Suicide, Euthanasia and Assisted Suicide.

True Happiness

Here I am in a sea of lies,
All I want to do is die
My life is nothing; my soul is gone
My mind is destroyed; Death is all I see
Blood flows from me
Tears fall, pain comes, chaos leaves
Calmness enters, then panic
Blood won't stop, feeling dizzy
World is spinning; Death comes
Hugs me in its cold warmth
The world won't miss me
I won't miss me
This is the end; my life is done
I finally know peace.

Nicholas (Nick) Funk. Age: 26…and still alive.

Here it becomes difficult. I believe people have the right to choose their own time to die. I price *quality* of life over *quantity*. But I also believe that people mistakenly choose death when there is hope that they cannot see – such as when depressed. I do believe strongly in personal freedom, but sometimes it is the best option for someone to step in and protect someone who is mentally ill, to allow at least a *chance* of recovery. However, the chancehas to be a *reasonable* one, pain removed (or at least minimised), and the life-to-be felt to be of value to the person who wishes to die.

Thus I am pro voluntary euthanasia and assisted suicide, even for people with mental illness (as an extreme last resort or under certain individual circumstances) – a controversial standpoint, and one that could fill another book. Euthanasia is the act of killing someone – with their consent – to end their suffering, usually when they are terminally ill. It is possible to argue that unipolar and bipolar disorder are terminal, though not to many people.

Euthanasia is different to helping someone to commit suicide, whereby the subject is killed by someone helping them. *Both* are illegal in the UK and most other countries. It is possible to undergo voluntary euthanasia in some countries, including for mental illness, even when no other treatments have been tried. For example, in Switzerland people may be prescribed a lethal dose of barbiturates that they then take. (Hence technically that is assisted suicide). It is also legal in the US state of Oregon. Again barbiturates are used. The person must be terminally ill, have less than 6 months to live, make a written application and two verbal requests, not be influenced by depression, two doctors must be convinced the request is serious and voluntary, the person must be aware of feasible alternatives and must then wait 15 days. The form they must fill in is now called "Request for Medication to End My Life in a Humane and Dignified Manner."

Recently, a descendent of Virginia Woolf committed suicide by walking in to a loch on a moonlit December night in Scotland. She had severe bipolar disorder, but actually killed herself when diagnosed with metastatic breast cancer, (hence: terminally ill). Should this woman have been assisted to die with more dignity and less pain? I would say (no I'd *shout*) yes. In the future I hope more people are given the option of voluntary euthanasia; and I hope that having a diagnosis of a mental illness does not automatically exclude someone from having this choice – though I fear it shall.

Should mental illness ever be regarded as a terminal illness? Just because it is not physically forcing a death that physicians cannot stop, the death of the mind and will is as sure a death as any other. One might argue that the association of suicide with mental illness and/or drugs and/or alcoholism means that the suicide cannot be rational. Yet chronically depressed, alcoholic, eating disordered addicted or schizophrenic people (in any combination of these) may decide that it is better to be dead than to continue living as they are.

The reason for my reservation is that I, for many years, attempted suicide repeatedly and wanted to die: I believed my decision was an informed one, and that I couldn't get well ever again. My suicide planning was cool, calm and collected. Yet all my attempts were impulsive, or done whilst avoiding thinking too much about what I was doing, when something just kind of snapped, and I rushed into dangerous behaviours or carefully prepared plans.

On *none* of those occasions do I consider myself to have been of sound mind. After years of thinking there was no cure, I eventually found something that worked, and I am now so grateful that all those attempts failed. Yet despite this, I would still fight for my right to choose my time of death, even if mentally ill. A decision not of sound mind can still be the best decision, and how many of us are of sound mind all the time anyway?

❧Extinction.

> "I'll not weep.
> I have no full cause of weeping; but this heart
> Shall break into a hundred thousand flaws
> Or ere I'll weep. O fool, I shall go mad."
>
> ❧ William Shakespeare, *King Lear* (Act IV, scene 1).

I have lived with the threat of my extinction for years; I still do. In fact, we all do, but many of us never think about it, never mind considering causing their own annihilation. My unfortunate experiences of suicide are that of a long-term suicidal person in agony, the attempted suicide survivor (many times over), the friend of far too many "successful" suicide victims, and the support and friend to many people now at risk, who sometimes attempt, and I dread finding that another one has gone.

All these doctors I see with their theories
Based on the half-truths my demons let me share.
They don't know I wrestle with these demons, & my thoughts, & their advice.
I can see they make sense in the real world but in my world,
Deep down where it matters only I have all the information.
Only I know the real threat to my life.
My one and only life before the extinction of Katy Sara Culling forever.
And the only person who truly sees how dangerous that risk is I,
The one person prepared to take a chance because after all,
It is my life we're 'playing' with here

❧ Katy Culling, age 24, diary.

You might think that such experience would have taught me too much about the suffering caused to those left behind to subsequently attempt to take my own life. It didn't: I could not see it. The thoughts of those I love and have lost choke me when I think of them, or something reminds me of them, and it happens *every* day.

I am drawn to people similar to myself, and therefore meet and make friends with people with mental illnesses. And the fact that I met huge numbers of people with mental illnesses in various hospitals means that I have an unusually high number of people close to me that have committed suicide; not all are mentioned here. There are also many people I befriended before they had any apparent illness that resulted in their suicide. Their absence is felt very strongly.

One person died from carbon monoxide poisoning from her car exhaust, in the days before cars came fitted with catalytic converters (I think I was about 10). Before I was 16, the brother of a girlfriend of mine "blew his brains out." I don't know how he got a gun in England. I remember his sister telling me about it, his family discovering him, his grey matter and blood sprayed over his bedroom walls. Depressed myself at the time, thinking of suicide, I swore never to depart this world in a messy fashion, but to be as considerate as possible considering someone would have to find my body. There is some weird logic to my thinking, if you consider it hard enough – I promise. That was the first rule I developed about how I would commit suicide. However the truth is, if I were desperate enough, I would use whatever was to hand.

Another school friend jumped, or fell, off a bridge into a river and drowned. He might have been hallucinating on LSD, and all involved preferred a verdict of accidental death. I also had two female friends who slashed their throats, both highly intelligent, capable people.

I personally know of seven people who attempted suicide by jumping from a height. One (Zee, who still lives) thankfully froze when it came to it; one died on the first attempt that I am aware of. The other five people who jumped survived and had horrific injuries that took months to recover from. One was in intensive care for a month. One broke his back. All five subsequently killed themselves. Three succeeded by jumping from somewhere higher the next time, two succeeded the next time by alternative methods (jumping in front of a train and self-strangulation).

Only one of those seven I did *not* know personally. I don't know if it was her first attempt or what her psychiatric history was, but I witnessed her death. In 2003 a girl who was between eighteen and twenty died in a horrific and violent way, right before my eyes. I empathised, I knew how she must have felt, and as I was still quite ill myself, I was actually jealous that ten years my junior, she had succeeded at something I had repeatedly failed at. That happened just one week after what I hope was my last suicide attempt, number 443, when I was the most depressed of my life.

I was in Derbyshire driving on a road that goes under a high bridge, thinking my usual thoughts, heading for home. I have no idea why I particularly noticed her, but in the distance I saw this dark-haired girl walk on to the bridge, straight towards the edge, and without a moment of hesitation, she just almost jumped over the rails, and ... stepped off. She did it as if it was nothing, almost if she expected to fly. She hit the ground feet first, smack, and crumpled like a compressing concertina. I almost felt her head crack as it impacted the road. I pulled over the car, and stopped to "help," call an ambulance and if needed, perform CPR.[42]

---

[42] Cardiopulmonary resuscitation.

For a moment, I thought her heart was still beating, her chest moved as if she was breathing, but I'm not sure if I didn't imagine that. Some of her head and brain was missing, and the lower half of her body was totally crushed. Fortunately she was unconscious. Moments later she had definitely stopped breathing.

I chose not to perform CPR. I have tortured myself about this decision, with thoughts that someone who was less sympathetic to her suicidal aim would have tried to keep her alive. I am, after all, trained to resuscitate, and people chose to resuscitate me when there was almost no hope. On that terrible day I did think, and I still think, that the girl dying before my eyes wouldn't want to live so severely disabled. But in honesty this is all moot. I knew at a glance that her injuries were lethal. She was so broken that there was nothing to save. I didn't see a point in pointlessly prolonging her death, and at least someone was with her when she died. I closed her eyes. I don't even know her name.

Other friends? I know one man who drank cyanide: a Chemistry student. I know of one young woman (doctor) who injected herself with a fatal dose of insulin, and another who tried the same, but lived. Another friend strangled herself days after being discharged from psychiatric hospital. One dear (Bipolar) friend of mine (a doctor) committed suicide at the end of 2005, just as another book of mine she had written in book was undergoing its final editing. I am still numb. It is the 5th anniversary of her suicide today.

Some of these people will be mentioned in the autobiography sections later, but most will not, because identifying when and where these incidents took place might lead people to identify the people who wish to remain anonymous.

Then of course, there was Declan – you will read more about him later. His death came as such a shock, and yet when

I think about the person he was, perhaps I should have expected it. *I don't think you ever really believe someone is going to kill themselves until it happens.* Maybe that is why people, including some health professionals are so flippant. In the autumn of 2003, Declan jumped in front of a high speed train near Oxford. He died instantly. I often wonder if he is at peace now, and hope that he is. (By peace, I do not mean in heaven, I mean that his suffering has ended, and he has found oblivion). I think of him frequently, and have a personal, private minute of silence for him, twice a year.

HOPE.

"Why do the bastards keep on bringing me back?"

ஐ Katy Culling, age 27, diary.

Thankfully they did.

Not everyone can be saved. Not everyone wants to be saved, and on a long enough timeline that really is an individual's prerogative, however much they love those they leave behind.

If you have lost someone, you have my unswerving empathy but remember that they did not intend to cause you pain, and they have ended their suffering. It is acceptable to consider that their pain has ceased and they have found peace, be that happiness or oblivion, without your feeling guilty.

One day the time may come where I choose not to be saved again. But for now, I am grateful for my life. I hope that I will always be able to remember that good follows bad ... eventually. I had a long depressive episode recently but did not once seriously consider suicide as an option. If you can find the strength within to hold on, or help someone else hold on, good times will come again.

Hold on. Don't give up.

Ch. 2. SELF-HARM: *Screaming silently in Agony.*

❧Introduction.

Masterpiece

Paint a picture with emotions of colour
Strokes of pain; dabs of beauty
My brush is my knife, my canvas my body
I start with my arms, making a pattern so beautiful

The pain is ecstasy. The hurts vanish
The joy comes. So I shall continue
Memories flood me
Rage comes, anger and hate

Soon I'll tear off my flesh; then burn it shut.
And devour the pills to be in my gut.
Fuck I'm beautiful. Blood and scars
Pain and rage; Life and death
I'm a masterpiece

❧Nicholas Funk. Age: 26

The term "self-harm" covers any act whereby a self-inflicted act that causes harm (i.e. it is exactly as it sounds). People cut, scratch, burn, stab, bloodlet, bang themselves, even break bones, overdose (on a variety of substances, to various levels of risk), swallow objects, insert objects, drink excessively, engage in less obvious self-harm like eating disordered behaviour, self-neglect, and/or engaging in other risky behaviours (e.g. driving dangerously) that are likely to cause harm. All of this is because they are in *deep emotional pain*, and it actually feels "better" to feel physical pain, or concentrate on a physical injury, than to cope with feelings that are overwhelming. It can feel better to see a wound (whether kept hidden, or shown to others), as such an injury can be tended to, cleansed, and looked after, or deliberately not looked after. *Emotional pain is far deeper and far more difficult to treat.*

Not all self-harm is suicidal. In fact most isn't.

Ideally the term self-harm should be used to describe situations where people self-harm for reasons other than to attempt suicide. However it is important to be aware that the commonly used term for attempted suicide and self-harm is "Deliberate Self-Harm" (DSH). All suicide attempts are classified by health professionals as "DSH," as they require, by definition an action that is harmful to yourself, where it just so happens that the motivation happens to be a desire to die.

I *object* to the term "deliberate" to describe suicide attempts and self-harm. For whilst it *is* true, that by definition, the harm is self-inflicted; the word "deliberate" suggests premeditation, a calculated choice, meditation, contemplation, manipulation, intention and conscious (therefore somewhat stupid) effort. Whilst some or all of those things may be true, they are not always; the act of self-harm is almost universally *unavoidable*, and has benefits outweighing the alternative (e.g. suicide, relief). Designating self-harm as "deliberate" assigns blame, and suggests the victim does not warrant appropriate, thoughtful help. In effect, assigning it as a "deliberate" act suggests that those whom self-harm "for purposes of manipulation do it on purpose," which goes hand in hand with the idea that it is only what they "deserve." This is decidedly unhelpful.

Other terms used include self-injury, self-mutilation, self-inflicted violence (SIV), self-cutting, parasuicide[43], and self-abuse. I will be using the term self-harm to refer to non-suicidal self-injury and the terms attempted suicide and suicide will be used where self-injury is the result of an attempt on life. People who self-harm are suffering intensely, but *not* usually attempting suicide. Instead they are trying to relieve the unbearable emotional pressure they are feeling and cannot cope with in another way. Indeed, sometimes self-harm can be the only act by which to *stop* actual suicide.

People that self-harm are discriminated against in society: approximately 50% if the population thinking that people whom self-harm are stupid and selfish. *Oh I am sorry, did I somehow inconvenience you when I drew the razor across my wrist to draw blood? Did you think that I did it just to piss you off or hurt you? Do you think I believed I would somehow transform the world into one filled with butterflies and daisies, in cartoon-like world where I can smack myself with a 10-tonne mallet and be fine?* Even when asking for help from friends and professionals, many prejudices exist. In part this is due to the understandable horror at seeing or knowing about the self-harm done; but that does not excuse how people are made to feel more worthless – only setting them up for more self-harm.

Here is an example of what happened to me when I injured my arm so badly I had to seek help:

> As I lived, got bored, hallucinated, but continued to bleed: I only once felt (mentally) strong enough to ask for help with my self-harm, and went to have stitches at the Accident and Emergency department in the John

---

[43] Parasuicide is technically another name for Attempted Suicide.

Radcliffe (JR) Hospital, Oxford. (I could not suture my left arm with one hand). I was not seeking attention or deliberately wasting time: I was ashamed. I know from my friends and working with self-harm victims that despite this being an everyday problem, covered in medical literature with massive insight; malpractice towards self-harm survivors is widespread: which is, in one word, *unacceptable*.

The one time I decided to get help I had been hallucinating, and, in fear, had harmed myself to quieten my panic and make the Dark Man (a hallucination) disappear: breaking my rule of cutting on my legs where I could self-suture. I went to A & E with three large, deep, and either rapidly oozing or pumping wounds on my left arm that I had been unable to stop bleeding. I had hit two arteries and one large vein (plus several small). Now there are arterial bleeds and different arterial bleeds. The two cuts that hit arteries were not large arteries. When I held my arm out for inspection the blood shot about 2 meters (not far really), pulsing across the room. That and the fact that it sprayed bright red up my College wall when I actually did it, is why I described it as arterial.

I was left sitting in the waiting room for a short time, but too long, surrounded by members of the public asking too many questions. I deposited a pool of blood beneath me on the floor. I really don't know where these incredible reserves of blood came from in my body. I began to feel immortal again, and displeased with that "fact". Waiting patients looked concerned and asked me what I had done. All they could see was a blood soaked towel and floor. I lied and said I had accidentally put my hand through a window; which seemed easier than the truth because I was tired and weak. (I now regret not telling the truth). "Ouch! How awful," they said, and nodded approvingly. Then I pretended to feel faint so that there would be no more questions. Then I really felt faint.

I was called though and seen by an Emergency Room Consultant. (I believe that's the same position as an Attending doctor in America). I suddenly found it hard to stand or walk. I did not bother to lie about "an accident" because it was bloody obvious to a professional that I had done this to myself, and it was impossible to ignore the multitude of older scars, most perfectly lined across my arm. He looked disapprovingly at me, and didn't speak to me other than a grunt to ask if I could move my fingers. He asked what I had cut myself with, and I replied in a quiet voice, "A sterile scalpel." He shot me a look of disgust.

I know I looked deathly pale, sweaty, unsteady; and I felt cold, dizzy, shaky, tremendously anxious and frightened; but I tried to appear calm. He did not give me any more chances to speak. I couldn't seem to get enough air, and saw shapes moving across the front of my eyes. I had trouble staying focussed. I was fainting/drifting when sitting, I had a woozy head, and my heart felt it was going to explode out of my chest.

It did not occur to me to ask them to check my blood pressure (or lack thereof). I did not ask them to test my haemoglobin. It didn't occur to me to ask for surgery to repair my sliced blood vessels or check I had not cut any nerves – I have never recovered feeling in my lower, left arm. Nor did it occur to me to ask that they should treat my fluid depletion, which must have been quite significant. It should have been abundantly overt that not only was I spraying blood around the clinical room, I had gone into hypovolaemic[44]

---

[44] Hypervolemia refers to a reduced amount of blood and blood components in the circulatory system – which can become life threatening if anoxia causes organs to fail. *Untreated shock is usually fatal.*

According to the National Institute For Clinical Excellence, "If uncorrected, hypervolemia will initially lead to inadequate perfusion and oxygenation of tissues and will subsequently cause permanent damage to vital organs and multiple organ failure, one of the major causes of death in trauma patients."

I estimate I lost about a litre that night, minimum.

shock, which needed treatment in the form of 0.9% saline or colloids, and a blood transfusion. But I received no treatment. Nor did anyone check my heart rate or breathing difficulties. My mind did not allow me to ask for their help, I was unable to care for myself properly – that was the job of the professionals.

The Consultant got up and left, and sent a nurse in who stuck about ten packets of steristrips on my arm – she just stuck them anyhow, all incorrectly, with no attempt to close my wounds. Even though the blood just washed them all away, she then proceeded to try to roll a bandage around my arm, which soaked through with blood in moments. Somehow I found the strength to suggest that I needed stitches, and she looked at me like I was fresh dog crap on her best carpet.

I didn't say it, but I knew I was being deliberately mistreated. Deemed unworthy. She ignored my request and proceeded with my blood-soaked bandage, so I pulled away my arm and *demanded* to see the Consultant. Where I found the strength to assert myself I do not know. What fears me is the question of how many people do not have the conviction to stand their ground, and suffer as a consequence. I suppose I was confidentenough that I was right, that they were wrong, that I knew the very least amount of physical medical treatment my wounds required, and that my self-harm didn't make me a bad person.

When, after a twenty-minute wait, the Consultant "graced" me again with his presence, I was *rather* pissed off. Fortunately this anger gave me the ability to say that I knew I needed stitches, although my brain was unable to connect with a need for other ways in which I needed to be treated properly. I just wanted the bleeding to stop. I dropped into the conversation I was studying medicine at Oxford; his ears perked up. I already had no respect for this man, who other doctors and nurses would look to, to see how to behave. *Great role model,* I thought: r*espect is earned, not demanded.* So I told him that I needed stitches: soon, where and why; and he just left the room without making eye contact. I spoke firmly but not impolitely: suppressing the part of me that wanted slap his face for his haughty disrespect.

The consultant reappeared with a large needle and 20ml syringe filled with anaesthetic, and stabbed me twice, briskly and carelessly, through two of the cuts and into my arm; totally ignoring the third wound, which was bleeding badly. He did not acknowledge me as a person at any juncture: unable to look at my face. I assume he was trying to make a point: whereas I just thought he was an arrogant wanker.

By this point the edges of my wounds were swollen and sore. Now I have been taught how to use the anaesthetic lignocaine (known as lidocaine in the USA). I know he could have used a smaller needle, and should have injected the lignocaine in a few areas, numbing the edges of all my cuts ready for the stitches. And he should have done it much more slowly; I have never seen so much lignocaine injected so fast and carelessly. (The faster it is injected, the more painful it is). The pain woke me up – where I had been floating away. He injected me twice *into* the cuts, which didn't numb the areas around the cuts properly, if at all. There was no suggestion of a psychiatric consultation – technically I was already under the care of the Warneford Hospital.

It was another fifteen minutes until a lovely nurse came to do my stitches. I had to ask her to properly numb my arm, which she did, obviously displeased with the Consultant and having to suture a wound that actually required surgery herself. Then she closed my skin with many sutures, bandaged it tightly, and we hoped for the best. I know she was uncomfortable with the poor treatment that I received;

but she was great, friendly and caring, not at all judgemental. Then I was allowed to walk out.

I should have complained. I *know* doctors are busy. I know Accident and Emergency is busy. Yes I physically caused my own injuries, but let's not forget that it was under the influence of several mental illnesses battling it out loudly in my head at the time. It was not my "fault" any more than someone who slips with a knife after a few glasses of wine, or who trips through a window when not paying attention, or indeed any other injury in any other circumstance. Self-harm does not make you a second-class citizen. *I was ill:* a fact all Emergency Department staff should know. *I could have died.* People without my medical training, or people less able to speak out about what they needed, would have been shamed, mistreated, scarred physically and mentally, and probably never returned for help again, even if a wound was life threatening. Indeed I never returned to the JR Emergency Department by choice. (Though I did return).

I received no psychological treatment.

If you work in emergency medicine, and cannot begin to comprehend why someone self-harms: educate yourself. No excuses just do it. Some health professionals are fantastic. Even if you are still inclined to think it is abominable, stupid and/or a waste of your precious time: you should still be professional. That means you are civil, respectful and provide the same standard of care you would anyone else; including consideration of the fact the person is likely to be highly distressed and vulnerable. Treating someone badly will *not* deter further self-harm; rather it will confirm to that person, already filled with self-hatred, that they are as worthless as they feared. And then they will self-harm more, and possibly die from suicide or untreated self-harm. Since my nightmare visit the NICE guidelines for such treatment have been written – I only hope they are followed.

One of the most difficult things combating self-harm is the total unknown figure of how many men, women and children are engaging in a form of self-abuse. It known that more women self-harm (or at least seek treatment for their injuries) than men, and that adolescents and people in their twenties are most at risk.

> "170,000 people a year attend emergency departments because they have self-harmed, of those an estimated 80,000 never receive a psychological assessment or follow up even though the risk of committing suicide after self-harming is 100 times greater than the average risk in the population."
>
> ❧Dr Tim Kendall, Consultant Psychiatrist and Co-Director of the NCC Mental Health.[45]

These figures include self-harm for non-suicidal and suicidal purposes, *for the UK only*. But most self-harm goes

---

[45] NICE Self-Harm guidelines (2004) see press release
http://www.nice.org.uk/page.aspx?o=214460

unreported making this a hidden problem: the real figures are unknown. For more information see recommended reading and the MIND information sheet.[46]

---

[46]http://www.mind.org.uk/Information/Booklets/Understanding/Understanding+Self-Harm.htm

✤Why?

> "There is a sacredness in tears. They are not the mark of weakness, but of power. They speak more eloquently than ten thousand tongues. They are messengers of overwhelming grief..."
>
> ✤ Washington Irving (1783-1859).

Self-harm seems so impossible to understand, whereas in actual fact, it has well-reasoned (if warped) motives behind it. As *every* case of self-harm is individual, it is difficult to generalise on this topic: indeed several reasons may cause a person to self-harm at a given time.

So why do you people start doing it? How do people discover that it is a "useful" tool to exploit? The answer is that it varies from person to person. I first cut myself out of a simple mixture of unconscious anger and depression, and conscious curiosity. I wasn't copying anyone and had never heard of self-harm at the time. Almost ten years passed between this first incident of cutting and the second.

People have described events such as cutting themselves by accident, and realising they felt a positive benefit from it, such as relief of tension. Some people cannot explain why they started. Some people no doubt read about it in the media and think they will try it. Television and films have also had an influence; a British soap opera had a character whoself-harmed by cutting herself, there were soon reports of a sharp increase in the number of girls and young women cutting themselves. Others learn self-harm techniques from the Internet.

❧ List of Reasons why people self-harm. (Not fully inclusive).

❖ To kill themselves.

❖ To appear to want to kill themselves: a "cry for help," seeking *needed* attention. Would you overdose or take a blade to your skin just to get attention? Many people who self-harm are ashamed, embarrassed, and attempt to conceal their behaviour from others. They shouldn't feel ashamed because they have *had* to self-harm for some important reason. Maybe it is the only way of communicating distress – and – unfortunately, in a world where the sickest people get treatment, it is a way of getting someone to sit up and take notice. When you are about to "lose the plot" and can't verbalise your feelings, it is possible to turn to self-harm so that it can articulate them for you.

❖ To *prevent* suicide. Self-harming with no intent of dying is often done in order to cope with agonising mental torment, and may epitomize the least damage that person can to do.

❖ As a result of many psychiatric illnesses, mainly post-traumatic stress disorder (as a result of abuse or an attack such as rape), borderline personality disorder, depression (of all kinds), eating disorders and body dysmorphic disorder.

❖ To numb unpleasant emotions by focussing attention on the act of self-harm and/or the pain caused by cutting, drinking, using drugs or burning etc. in order to make unpleasant memories and feelings go away *temporarily*. Forcing physical pain upon yourself forces you to focus on the immediate pain, rather than past psychological pain. A private tightrope that some people try to walk to cope with unbearable emotional pain: anger, self-hatred, guilt, Depression, fear, loneliness, emptiness etc. I describe it as a tightrope because some people self-harm with no intention of dying, and then do actually die as a result of their injuries.

❖ Some people inflict pain in order to feel something – feeling anything; even pain is preferable to feeling nothing, when feeling nothingness, and being emotionally numb for a number of reasons. It can serve as a reminder that the person is "alive."

❖ Some people injure themselves as a form of reassurance that they will bleed, will bruise, and will burn, when they fear an eternity of pain or even feel immortal. (This tends to be during psychosis or mania, especially when suicidal).

❖ Oblivion. Some people seek temporary oblivion either by self-harming to block out all feelings, or, by a method that is becoming alarmingly more common (based on the people I know who self-harm), taking overdoses of sedatives to knock themselves out. The drugs used to do this. (Indeed some people mistakenly overdose on drugs that have no sedative affect, but which do their body harm) but all are dangerous, potentially lethal instantly, and will do long-term damage to the body. Alcohol continues to be abused as a form of seeking oblivion.

❖ To focus attention on blood – some people "enjoy" seeing themselves bleed.

❖ Some people do "enjoy" pain – the reasons behind this are very complicated, and by no means applies to many people who self-harm.

❖ Purging. Some people believe that if they lose blood they will lose weight or change their body, (these people tend to have Eating Disorders or Body Dysmorphic Disorder).

❖ To focus on taking care of a physical wound rather than an emotional one.

❖ To prove to themselves or others that they are ill and deserving of treatment. Common in people with low self-esteem.

❖ To relieve stress, with a release of tension often described as a benefit following self-harming behaviour.

❖ To feel in control. Common in Eating Disorders.

❖ To punish themselves. Common in people who have been abused.

❖ Some people are believed to get addicted to the high they feel, caused by the release of endorphins, the body's natural opiate that occurs when they self-harm. Frequency and severity of their self-harm has to escalate to get this same high, as tolerance grows like in any addiction. Some people may argue self-harm is not addictive as it does not produce cravings or withdrawal; however I say these qualities are very much present, psychologically.

❖ I sometimes self-harmed to abuse my medical knowledge and training, for the reason that I was angry that I had not been allowed to qualify and practice as a medical doctor due to my ill health. I used medical equipment, anaesthesia, blood-giving sets, scalpels, performing if you will, my own strange surgery. There will be more about this later. I know I am not alone to use bloodletting equipment, but as yet, I have not heard of or encountered anyone surgically cutting their body as I did for the purposes of self-harm. I have no grandiose opinions about this clinical, antiseptic, anaesthetised self-surgery of mine; it may not be a well-documented practice, but I doubt very much that I am alone.

❖ Motives are unknown by the person at the time, or that are unconscious.

❖ Motives that are as of yet, unheard of.

Because of a feeling that no one was listening to me, I fell in to the trap of feeling I had to prove my distress and earn help by doing more and more dangerous things with my acts of self-harm. I had to cut deeper, lose more blood. I used local anaesthetic to numb myself so I could cut really deeply and find arteries. I enjoyed the time it took me to clean up and suture my wounds. I bloodlet using blood giving sets, literally watching the blood pour out of me – I was out of control and hospitalised at this time but still found ways to do it. I cycled in and around buses with a death wish, overdosed and so on. *I was yelling at full volume, although it seemed silently, in all of the ways I could manage, for someone to help me, and I was getting nowhere.*

My messages, including self-harm, were clear but not acted upon. In my case, I then mostly abandoned self-harm for attempted suicide, obviously a dangerous pathological progression that went ignored for far too long. My attempts at suicide were never a cry for help. I intended them to work and therefore didn't require any help, nor need to prove anything to anyone. Some of my suicidal acts became more dangerous as my distress and knowledge grew, some were less dangerous depending on what dangerous items I could or could not get hold of.

❧Forms of self-harm.

The most common form of self-harm *without* lethal intent is cutting skin, commonly on the forearm and upper legs with knives or razors. But there are people who cut themselves in other places, or indeed eventually in every place on their body over a period of time. I've noticed that usually the face is left unscathed. Victims of sexual abuse might cut their upper thighs, genitalia or breasts because these body areas represent traumatic experiences to them. People with Eating Disorders might cut their stomach because they are obsessed that it is ugly and fat and they want to punish themselves. Some even try to suck fat out.

The list of ways to self-injure is fairly endless. Many people use more than one method. Some people swallow various liquids such as detergent, or take overdoses of almost any medication available, not to kill themselves but to make themselves feel ill as a punishment, or to sleep in order to feel less emotional pain. Usually overdosing is done with some lethal intent, even though damage can sometimes be minimal. Of course, some overdoses kill. The most common form of self-harm that is suicidal is overdosing.

Another forms of self-harm is risky sex, which might mean going with someone potentially dangerous who could beat, hurt or kill you, not taking precautions against HIV and AIDS, other transmitted diseases, and pregnancy. This behaviour might be repeated again and again, just as with other forms of self-harm.

Some people swallow things in order to cause pain, and possibly get attention from doctors where they require x-rays or even surgery, and therefore feel looked after. (Some might suggest this borders on Munchausen's Syndrome[47]). Things that I personally have seen swallowed are open safety pins, other pins, razor blades, sewing needles, syringe needles, broken cups and plates, glass, dirt, elastic bands and faeces. Sometimes large quantities of one of these, all within the confines of a psychiatric ward. I suspect the full list of items swallowed is far more extensive.

I am aware that some people use alcohol as a form of self-harm. They are aware that it makes them very ill, and yet continue to drink. Drink is also commonly used before an act of self-harm, as an aid to the actual act, increasing impulsivity, aggression (towards self) and to anaesthetise, albeit not very well. Some people who do not self-harm when sober will self-harm when drunk, sometimes most precariously; and sometimes after blacking out and having no memory of what they did. Some people start to drink knowing they cannot stop once started; knowing that this puts their life at risk, not because of the alcohol per se but because of how they behave when drunk. One of my best friends used to do this.

The same can be true of people using street-drugs. Of course, both alcohol and drugs can be overdosed on, which can result in suicide, with or without intention of dying. When alcohol and drugs are abused during suicidal or self-harm events, they increase the potential lethality of the event, and some people die or are injured as a result of a "decision" they made whilst under the influence.

Another form of self-harm is burning. For example holding an iron, a pan, or similar to your skin, again arms are common, but this is not exclusive. Other people might burn

---

[47] Munchausen's Syndrome is a serious factitious mental disorder whereby the victim makes-up symptoms, or self-induces symptoms that require medical attention, out of a desire to feel cared for.

themselves with matches, lighters or lit cigarettes. Burning is particularly painful, and can lead to badly healing wounds, infections and scarring. I once tried it with my cigarette on a particularly bad night of hallucinating – it was agonising and I still have the scars.

Some people hit or bang themselves to cause bruising, some people even doing enough damage to break bones. Some people try to act recklessly, such as on the road, and are in car and bike accidents causing themselves harm, though this is an obvious area where the question of whether the behaviour was a suicide attempt should definitely be asked. The same is true if someone jumps a height and is injured, or crashes their head through a window. Is that self-harm without intent to die, or attempted suicide? Each case is individual and can only be assessed as such.

Just as eating disorders can be described as a slow form of suicide, they could equally be described as self-harm. Laxative abuse is self-harm and can be very painful, slow starvation, bingeing and vomiting are all self-harm also. Just as cutting with a knife, these forms of self-harm are coping strategies, giving the sufferer something positive in return for the harm done. Perfectionism is a common trait in anorectics, as it is in self-harmers. Apart from physical harm the eating disorder does to the sufferer day after day, other forms of self-harm are common in people with eating disorders.

❧ The Risks.

Apart from the obvious risk of death, self-harm is exceedingly dangerous. The quantity, severity, frequency and type of self-harm are important considerations. There are limits to the amount of self-harm you can do before you end up in an institution, but often you can go frighteningly far before this happens, far enough for the damage to your body to be permanent. *There is no such thing as a "safe" overdose*, even if you have used the same amount before. Burns and cuts lead you open to very nasty infections. Cutting makes it possible to cut arteries or veins causing a large loss of blood, making the person ill, anaemic, or even leading to death. There is a risk are that you might cut tendons requiring surgery to prevent loss of movement, and risk of cutting nerves which can lead to loss of sensation – Personally, I cannot feel the inside of my left arm.

All cuts lead to scarring, deep cuts to the worst scarring. Scars are for life and people noticing them usually react as you might expect them to react if you were a purple spotted Martian with hair like Medusa. (Sometimes I find, coping with self-harm requires humour, even though there is actually nothing funny about it). I do not mean to criticise the general public, such disbelief and embarrassment is a natural, if uneducated reaction; but what people actually understand does need changing. That will happen when more and more sufferers speak up.

A major, often forgotten risk of self-harm is the misunderstanding you open yourself up to in society. This is an extreme misunderstanding that may affect you in many derogatory ways. Scars can prevent you getting a job (though some employers will not admit to that). There are certain jobs where this is more likely to be a problem: nursing being the prime example.

It has been my experience that cutting, or any form of self-harm that results in highly visible blood loss is distressing to onlookers such as fellow patients and professionals. It is a normal human reaction to feel horrified at the self-inflicted pain and bloody-mess. Although I have self-harmed, I react with instinct, with horror when I see someone self-harm, a natural gut-reaction to the situation.

I think that occasionally this reaction can be misread by the self-harming individual making them think that they are communicating with others, expressing their pain, and getting care and attention that they are in desperate need of. This is true of recent wounds, not just ones performed publicly. I know many people who self-harm, only one guy I knew called Zee did it publicly – sometimes. Unfortunately, despite desperate depression, Zee was eventually labelled as unmanageable and untreatable, and got *less* help. He didn't help matters by wearing a specially made T-shirt that said

"Dr T******
is a fucking
wanker
psychiatrist!"

(That got him discharged from hospital – so I am told).

Other people seek help in a less dramatic ways with self-harm, but it is still intensely distressing to people supporting the self-harmer, and even distressing to professionals. My Oxford therapist's face would drain of all colour, her eyes filled with pain – and that was just if I had my arm wrapped in a bandage. Remember that though not all self-harm is to get professional or family consideration; some is used for this exact purpose. You will get attention whether you want it or not.

"Attention seeking" is a term used in a most derogatory sense, as some sort of terrible or shocking label. Whereas I think that people who have to go to these extremes to get someone's awareness *are in dire need of help* and such inappropriate labelling is counter-productive and cruel. Attention seeking is not "bad," for these people it is *essential*. Unfortunately, the help you receive may be far removed from what you want or need. There are other ways, far less painful, less filled with despair and utter self-hatred to get attention if you want it. Try going to a public shopping centre totally naked, or even in a skimpy bikini should do it, (especially if you are a bloke).

I suggest we rethink the term "attention seeking," and stop using it in such a bad light. We should think of it as a necessary action from someone in severe distress rather than something we think of with such condescension, and misunderstanding. Attention seeking can be *necessary*, and it can be *good*.

❧Ways to help, and ways not to help.

> "How dreadful knowledge of the truth
> can be when there's no help in the
> truth."
>
> ❧Sophocles

Self-harm by definition, is *never* safe and is rarely completely secret. However, harm can and should be minimised. At times medical staff doesn't want to make a big deal out of self-harm because they do not want to "reward" people with attention, and actually this encourages people to repeat the self-harm, often with greater severity, in order to get help or feel deserving. Treating people who self-harm in a degrading fashion, or as unimportant, can be the result. This leaves people screaming for help at ever-increasing volumes, in unhealthy ways, and undoubtedly some people die or get more ill before they get eventually get help.

Those people that come forward for help with any self-harm should be considered to be communicating their distress, or possibly showing unwillingly that their self-harm is so out-of-control they have harmed themselves so badly to force them to seek medical attention, and need help. Even self-harm that is not medically life-threatening maybe meant very seriously. A person with a small, non-life threatening cut on the wrist, is in their own way asking for help, and might walk out the hospital doors and jump straight under a bus. All self-harm is serious; all is blaring out about emotional turmoil, and should be taken seriously. Unfortunately this is not how many people are treated; when they seek medical attention many people describe feeling mistreated and degraded. I am generalising:

there is help out there and there are professionals who understand.

Suicide attempts should not be confused with other self-harm, but attempted suicide should not whimsically be ruled out: a person who self-harmed should be assessed for further risk. Self-harm *may* be a suicide attempt, irrespective of whether the self-harm is actually life threatening. The medical seriousness of any act of self-injury should not be the only fact taken into consideration when determining any form of intent or distress to that person, or treatment offered.

An evaluation also needs to be made by talking to the individual and considering why the person did it, what they hoped to achieve, and checking for previous medical records of self-harm/suicide attempts. Medical staff should treat *all* self-injury with consideration, so as not to make that person feel stupid, ineffective, unworthy and misunderstood. This should be in accordance with the UK, 2004, NICE guideline, *New guideline to standardise care for people who self-harm*, that was set up to try to improve awareness and care given to those who self-harm.[48]

ᴥThe basic NICE Guideline for people who self-harm from press release:

> ❖ People who have self-harmed should be treated with the same care, respect and privacy as any patient and that healthcare professionals should take into account the distress associated with self-harm.

---

[48] NICE - National Institute of Clinical Excellence, National Health Service, UK.
Website: http://www.nice.org.uk/ See press release at http://www.nice.org.uk/page.aspx?o=214460

❖ Appropriate training should be provided for staff coming into contact with people who self-harm.

❖ Emergency room staff who may be involved in the care of people who have self-poisoned should ensure that activated charcoal is immediately available at all times.

❖ All people who have self-harmed should be offered a preliminary psychosocial assessment at triage (or at the initial assessment in primary or community settings) following an episode of self-harm. Assessment should determine a person's mental capacity, their willingness to remain for further (psychosocial) assessment, their level of distress and possible presence of mental illness.

❖ People who have self-harmed should be offered treatment for the physical consequences of self-harm, regardless of their willingness to accept psychosocial assessment or psychiatric treatment.

❖ All people who have self-harmed should be assessed for future risk of self-harm and/or suicide and the key psychological characteristics associated with risk, in particular depression, hopelessness and continuing suicidal intent should be identified.

Many people do not seek or treatment for their problem or their injuries. Often self-treatment is done silently, alone, at home, even if medical attention is needed. The way to combat self-harm long-term is to understand what triggered it initially, what continues to trigger it, and alternative ways to cope with overwhelming emotions. As the NICE guideline states, a full physical, psychological and social assessment should be offered; and if it is not, you are within your rights to ask why not. (This is why it is often helpful to take a friend or relative with you, as standing up for yourself when you feel so worthless is very difficult). These forms of help should be initiated by the Emergency Department where you are seen, by your GP, or by other professionals you seek help from (such as your psychiatrist if you have one).

If you cannot talk to a professional, at least talk to someone whom you trust; it is important not to feel alone. It is all very well to say that you have the right to expect "an atmosphere of respect and understanding." But I hate to admit that currently: this is fairly often *not* the case. (Taking nothing away from professionals who are wonderful and empathic, others can treat you like utter shit). If you have trouble getting help, MIND recommend that you contact the Patient Advice and Liaison Services[49] You are entitled to a second opinion and to change your General Practitioner. You have a right to change your GP, if you wish, or you may see another GP at the same practice.

For those people that do present with an injury (or several) there is the immediate need for emergency treatment for the

---

[49] PALS (UK only) are listed in your phone book under the local NHS Trust.

physical harm done. You can walk into an Emergency Department at any time. Often doctors there have not the time to do much more than treat any immediate danger, and recommend a psychiatric follow up. According to the NICE guideline, (in the UK) you should get proper assessment and help should you choose to take it. You may choose not to – unless you are considered to need compulsory treatment. Some doctors assume that a serious injury means you are psychotic, which is often false.

I have found that some emergency room doctors can be rather passive-aggressive (or even aggressive as I described on my visit – which was prior to the NICE guidelines being written) towards people who self-harm, and therefore strongly feel that training about self-harm should be increased and improved as suggested in the NICE guideline. Maltreatment of sufferers, mental and physically just maintains the circle of self-harm and destruction.

There are, of course, many good (excellent) doctors and nurses out there, but amongst the good doctors and nurses, only a handful have treated me in a way that I felt was helpful and left me feeling dignified about self-harm, suicidal or not. These people behaved in such an empathic, non-judgemental fashion that it makes me doubly angry that there are other professionals that treat you badly. It is not necessary, and it is certainly not helpful.[50] What upsets us (those of us who self-harm, used to self-harm, and/or have psychiatric illness) is the INCONSISTENCY of care that is offered.

It would be unfair to solely blame the professionals. Patients may not want further investigations. I have sat in an emergency room, had my arm stitched after a life-threatening

---

[50] See the autobiographical sections of this book for more details – good and bad – about what it is like to be a Self-Harm and Attempted Suicide patient being treated in a GP's surgery, an Emergency room and on a psychiatric ward.

self-inflicted wound, (which was actually attempted suicide that did not work, I got bored, and I could not stitch my own arm with one hand, nor stop the blood with pressure). The doctor said I would need to have a psychiatric consult before he wanted me to leave. I said "no," and walked out. They should have stopped me, some professionals probably would have stopped me, others are just too bored, tired, fed-up, angry or don't care. My point is: do not expect to be saved; your life is in your own hands.

If your self-harm is severe, certainly if it is life-threatening, you will be referred to a crisis intervention team or psychiatric hospital where you may be required to stay, with or without your agreement. (Possibly following a stay on a medical ward to stabilize your medical i.e. physical condition). I have a tendency to push people to see how far I can go. I don't know why and I don't recommend you follow my example. One day you find that they *do* stop you from leaving, and you lose your freedom. Trust me that it is quite a shock to the system.

Again, the level of self-harm required causing such involuntary detention and big crisis meetings varies. One day you could be told you are on a 28-day section for assessment as a suicide risk, the next day you are kicked out because someone more ill needs the bed. It happens. Such terrible *inconsistency* is unacceptable.

Treating anyone who deliberately self-harms is difficult, particularly if they do not want it because self-harm is serving their purposes "well." Many also do not feel they deserve help for a self-inflicted problem. The injury is self-inflicted, but the reasons behind it are not: a very important distinction. You might say, "Well I self-harm because of my anorexia, and that is my fault, I choose to be anorectic." But anorexia is not a choice, whatever the cause, if you go back far enough, a person who self-harms is a victim – and a survivor – as self-harm is a form of survival.

Treatment needs to be individualised and may well begin with harm minimisation, or even with persuading the self-harmer to clean and dress their wounds to prevent infection. Remember a person who self-harms will undoubtedly have low self-esteem, and preventing infection or reducing severity of scars by good first aid practice is a good start.

Self-harm is caused by other problems in life, rather than being a diagnosis in its own right. (Although if it becomes addictive; the addiction needs treating also). In order to treat self-harm, the reasons behind the behaviour need to be addressed, usually in psychotherapy or counselling, and with medication if a person has a diagnosable mental illness that would benefit from drug treatment, as prescribed by a GP or Psychiatrist.

Psychological treatments are usually of great benefit. CBT is a form of psychotherapy where people learn to self-hatred, place past events in the past and move on with their life. It is possible to learn better ways to cope with powerful emotions such as sadness, pain, anger and loneliness. It is also possible to change core beliefs, such as that you are worthless, or deserve punishment. Psychoanalytical treatments are forms of psychotherapy whereby issues in the person's life (e.g. childhood trauma) are looked at in more detail. Personally, I feel CBT can help you sort out your psychological issues well enough without becoming too Freudian and thinking on issues that might be too painful to re-live. But that is just my opinion for my personal situation.

The approach of ignoring self-harm works in a few cases, but that must be the responsibility of professionals who have ensured they understand the person's they are treating very well, and have built up knowledge of that person *over time* to lead them to suspect reasons other than those admitted to, or for whom other methods have failed. Ignoring self-harm should only be done under careful watch (i.e. in serious cases, whilst hospitalised). I can only think of one person in my 25 years of mental illness for whom this approach half-worked.

There are many self-harm organisations around the world, many on the Internet (see the back of this book for recommendations) that are understanding and battling to improve all forms of care for people who self-harm.

❧Dangers of the Internet.

With a warning that emotions tend to run high on these websites, I direct you to the Internet to read about self-harm, harm minimisation, and to find self-help groups. There are pro self-harm websites where continuing to self-harm is the normal practice, which I feel are better to avoid if you can. Whilst I understand that for some people, self-harm is a necessary coping strategy, it is not a healthy one; I cannot not encourage it. There are some great pro recovery websites that will supply you with information and contacts for support. There are also many internet forums, although I find *some* of these to be filled with highly distressed people, in need of help, unwilling/unable to seek it, with several threats of suicide daily. I do not condemn these forums, just warn you that you might not find calming support, rather you may find a world of stress.

A very real warning I have, based on the fact I was a member of a self-harm website for a long time, is that the support is often limited and you must go to these sites with realistic expectations. You may very well find a lot of help, but help is not always available 24 hours a day, and on some sites there may be a policy of non-intervention. Yes, I mean it is policy to allow members to die even if they ask for help.

I was banned from a self-harm website (and sacked as a volunteer for them), because I called the emergency services and saved a pregnant 17-year old girl's life. She, posted a suicide note on the forum saying she had changed her mind; then privately told me what she had taken, then passed out, and I knew it was highly dangerous. When the Network was questioned immediately following my ban:

Website member: *"So Katy Sara was banned because she saved *******'s life."*

Network Moderator: *"In a nutshell, yes."*

So my warning is: do not expect to post suicide notes and be saved (on any site, not just self-harm sites). You might be; you might not. Even if I got banned from a hundred sites, I would do the same thing again, and fortunately many websites have the policy that whilst they cannot be expected to intervene, there is no "punishment" of members who do intervene to help others, indeed helping fellow members is smiled upon. Websites might be poorly regulated and are unpredictable – taking nothing away from many excellent sites that there are out there.

❧ Survivor story: The Stepmother

Catherine began to self-harm following physical, emotional and sexual abuse, together with neglect. She still does not understand why she chooses to continue hurting herself in the way her abuser hurt her. Be warned, this is a profoundly disturbing story, told most bravely and with great emotion…

The Stepmother

> I'm lying on the bed and you can't see my face: thank the devil for small blessings. As my mind fades in and out between now and seven years ago, I look down at the crescent-shaped scars on the back of my hand, but suddenly they're bleeding again. And there's blood on my nails. And my attention is jerked away to a sudden pain in my rear. I refuse to look up; I know what's going on. The stiff plastic cord isn't going to get any softer with my gaze, all because I refused to get in the shower again?
>
> I know you like the water pouring over us, forming a thin film in what space there is between our bodies. Maybe that's why I said no? Because I knew you wanted it? I dig my nails in again as the metal tips strike my young skin. This will leave scars; I know it. I will see them in seven years and tell myself they are stretch marks, but I won't ever be able to fool myself for long. I'm disillusioned. I get tired of the hair dryer cord and relent to another shower. With you. I don't want

to look at you, but you tell me you love me and suddenly everything's all right again. I know you love me; I love you too. I hug you, the clean skin of my nine-year-old arms skidding across your almost-thirty-year-old stomach.

And you kiss my mouth and let your hands roam as you sit down in the water. You tell me to touch you; I do so willingly, since you've reminded me again and again that this is how people show love. But I can't tell anyone, you warn, or they'll get jealous. And then people will be upset with me because I'm getting your love and nobody else is, not even your husband... my father.

So you show me pictures and read me stories, and you lie on the bed with me and we play with each other. But not just playing like I do with my friends: this is a special kind of playing. Other friends don't matter. I have you and you have me. You put my head between your legs and it tastes salty, and sometimes there's an extra burst at the end if I do good. And then you say you love me so much it's almost like you're my mother, so you have me do what babies do. And you say you like it, but something feels wrong. It felt wrong that first time you put your hand between my legs, but you told me it was okay. You tangle my fingers in your hair and pull my head from your chest; now it's time for you to show me how much you love me. You drag your nails down my skin and it makes my spine shiver. I get that urgent feeling again, that this shouldn't be happening feeling, and it's pounding more fiercely than my heart, but you tell me that's what love feels like. And I believe you. You're the adult. You know the ways of the world; I'm lucky to be getting such attention from you. I'm flattered that I'm the one you've chosen to love; the simple act of pleasing you makes my life worthwhile.

A year later, the shower is over and you want to play again. "I'm tired," I say. But you don't care; you want to play. I protest and you raise the brush, and I lower my head in submission, as I always do, when I realize, I'm sick of this. Hurt me if you want. So you pull out a needle. I've been bad. I must be punished. You pull my arm towards you and sting my skin; I jerk away and a thin red line appears. It gets thicker and thicker as I watch; even better, she says, deeper than I meant, but it should teach you a lesson. Tears well up in my eyes like the blood on my arm…this is the first time you've broken the skin. I doubt your intentions for the first time, but you see it in my eyes and hug me to your bare chest. You insist it had to be done, that I couldn't be let go without being taught a lesson. And any resistance melts away, and I nod my head. I know.

The needle became a regular thing, and I think you even used a knife once. But it was mostly the hair dryer cord and the hairbrush, until one day... I see boxes, you unpack some and find the front of a drawer. It doesn't have the handle in it yet. And you hide it in your jacket and set the rest up, and you make me help. About thirty seconds into it you tell me you're hot and you take off your clothes, and you instruct me to do the same. It's finished and we're tired. What we need is a long hot shower. So we hug and we kiss and we dry each other off, and you writhe all over the bed as I hug your leg. And you tell me to give you a haircut; you want to look nice for me down there. I wash your hair and cut it and dry it. You make me set it in curlers and distract you from that area while it sets. So I move up higher; I can't help myself, you're pulling my arms. And I sit on your stomach and put my head next to yours, and you lick my lips and tell me I'm beautiful.

He comes home. You shove me upstairs and tell me to go in the bathroom so he won't see me naked. You wrap yourself in the towel we shared so you can say you just got out of the shower. And he notices you've put the desk together, but you complain that a piece is missing. The drawer front you've hidden in your jacket. So Dad sends a letter of complaint and they ship it to us, but not before I've found why you hid that thick square of wood.

...The heavier it is, the more it hurts.

Catherine McCarthy. Age 21, (2010).
Location: United States of America.
Dedication: With thanks to Dr. Karen Bardenstein.

✎Survivor story 2: The experience of self-harm without suicidal intent.

In the beginning, it might have been a cry for help. However, as the years went on, the cutting still released the tension, but I began to lose the bad after-feeling associated with it. The scars no longer trouble me. The lines, diagonal, vertical and hatched onto my arms and belly. The star I carved on my arm, which I thought, "oh, it'll look cool." The words, "always second best," and "I love Fiona T?" scrawled in my best (or worst) left-handed style.

The first time it happened it took great determination, and I guess a lot of emotion and adrenaline. No matter how upset I was, and get, it always hurt(s), but there are times when all the tension, hurt, emotion and loneliness, numbs the pain like an ice pack.

The hiding really bothered me; the effect of me changing my shell appearance, at first drove me to be more reclusive. My friends backed away, and still do, because they don't understand. Even though I felt my friends were distant, I always had certain people. They maybe weren't the same people, but the majority of the time, there was somebody that I could share the pain and the mutilation with. Eventually, I stopped hiding.

I cut out and kept some articles concerning a girl from near here who killed herself in 2001. It really makes me agitated when people assume I'm suicidal. Yes, I know that there are plenty of people who change their bodies in this way who feel suicidal. But it should never be a "cut and paste" label. In my view, there is something almost artful in self-harm and suicide: the beautiful expression of true feelings. Often, it is a shame when people hide inside a shell, a disguise. At the other end of the spectrum, there are the ones like me who let it show, very graphically and often as a final statement.

Gordon Harper. Age 24 (2010).
Glasgow, Scotland, UK.
Dedication: *To Fiona T and Dina Tcheremissina (my Russian/Latvian London friend) You will never know what you mean to me.*

❧HOPE.

> "Write till your ink be dry, and with your tears
> Moist it again, and frame some feeling line
> That may discover such integrity."
>
> ❧William Shakespeare, *The Two Gentlemen of Verona* (Act 3, scene 2).

Let go of the anger and the pain. I had, note I <u>had</u> a severe self-harm history for suicidal and non-suicidal reasons. If I can beat it, so can you. Understand the cause(s) - depression, mania, psychosis, loss, anger, jealousy, anxiety etc. and you will find that you can control the behaviour. Seek out cognitive behavioural therapy or dialectical behavioural therapy and find a supportive network online (where people are trying to abstain from self-harm), talk to your doctor – you may well be depressed and need antidepressants.

If you do self-harm make sure you are aware of signs of infection (redness, heated area, rash that spreads, puss) and seek immediate attention – you need antibiotics, and I'm sure you rather take them orally at home than end up on a drip in hospital for a couple of nights.

I managed to quit self-harming after over 15 years of being addicted to it, so can you.

❧CONCLUSION.

> "There is in this (melancholic) humour, the very seeds of fire. In the day-time they are affrighted still by some terrible object, and torn in pieces with suspicion, fear, sorrow, discontents, cares, shame, anguish, etc., as so many wild horses, that they cannot be quiet an hour, a minute of time, but even against their wills they are intent, and still thinking of it, they cannot forget it, it grinds their soul day and night, they are perpetually tormented.
>
> In the midst of these squalid, ugly, and such irksome days, they seek at last, finding no comfort, no remedy in this wretched life, to be eased of all by death, to be their own butchers, and execute themselves."
>
> ❧ Excerpt from *The Anatomy of Melancholy* by Robert Burton. (1577–1640). Clergyman and scholar. Born in Leicestershire, educated at Oxford.

Suicide remains a terrible problem and one that needs much more research in to it. All those thousands of deaths each year, one million a year, and an ever increasing number of young deaths...

Unfortunately the world is not quite ready to understand self-harm. However I happily wear short sleeves shirt, my left arm exposed. I don't do it to antagonise, but nor do I feel I should hide. It's impossible not to notice my self-harm. I scrutinize for the smallest reaction, and sometimes there's a big reaction, sometimes people do an embarrassed double take, some people literally do not see what is under their noses. Sometimes somebody who doesn't know me looks at my arm and I look straight back at them. So much has happened that I just don't care anymore. It's quite liberating. If asked, I explain I was ill, and that I am not embarrassed. I am not proud, I do not claim them as my "battle scars," but I refuse to be ashamed. I will not hang my head in shame.

As for suicide, and my total of 443 attempts, well that number has not increased in eight years now, and I am hopeful it will remain that way, though it is hard work, requires medication and regular liaising with my doctors and psych nurse. I handed over my intended exit route to Prof Heun my psychiatrist to hopefully keep me safe. But there are so many ways… Familiarise yourself with the NICE guidelines so you know what to ask for should you end up in the Emergency Room.

Keep safe, and remember when dark times strike, HOLD ON, they will pass.

Useful Websites and books

My website: http://www.katysaraculling.com/

Alcoholics Anonymous (Global).
Website: http://www.aa.org/

American Psychiatric Association
Website: www.psych.org/

American Psychological Association
Website: www.apa.org/

American Association for Suicidology
4201 Connecticut Avenue, Suite 408
Washington, D.C. 20008
(202) 237.2280
(202) 237.2282 (Fax)
Email: Info@suicidology.org
Website: www.suicidology.org

Befrienders International (now maintained by the Samaritans).Suicide prevention worldwide, with 31,000 volunteers in over 40 countries).
Website: http://www.befrienders.org/index.htm

Mind (National Association for Mental Health) UK based
0845 7660163
Website: http://www.mind.org.uk/

Narcotics Anonymous (Global).
Website: http://www.na.org/

National Alliance for the Mentally Ill
Website: www.nami.org/

National Institute of Mental Health (USA).
Website: http://www.nimh.nih.gov/

NICE: National Institute of Clinical Excellence, National Health Service, (UK).
Website: http://www.nice.org.uk/

The Samaritans
Website: www.samaritans.org/
Phone: 08457 90 90 90 (UK).

Recover your Life (from self-harm).
http://www.recoveryourlife.com/

SANE (UK)
Website: http://www.sane.org.uk/

SOS: Survivors of Suicide:*forrelatives and friends* left behind after a loved one commits Suicide. Tony Salvetore's website which is described as "A site for those who have experienced suicide loss and those who want to know more about suicide and its aftermath."
Website: http://lifegard.tripod.com/

Oxford University's Centre for Suicide Research
Website: http://cebmh.warne.ox.ac.uk/csr/

For medical, mental and physical advice – e.g. following self-harm. (UK based only)

NHS Direct.
Phone (24 hours) 0845 4647
Website: www.nhsdirect.nhs.uk

Recommended Books and journals

Dark Clouds Gather (2008) Katy Sara Culling. A brutally honest tale of bipolar disorder leading to a total breakdown, serious anorexia and bulimia, brutal self-harm, 443 suicide attempts but eventual recovery of sorts.

Too Good For This World (2010) Katy Sara Culling. Two of the authors in this book telling their story ultimately commit suicide, others talk about it.

Night Falls Fast (2000) Kay Redfield Jamison – superb book, highly recommended.

Suicide and Attempted Suicide (2000) Keith Hawton and Kees van Heeringen

Suicide and Attempted Suicide (1999) Geo Stone

The Anatomy of Melancholy (2001)

No Time to Say Goodbye: Surviving the Suicide of a Loved One by Carla Fine

The Savage God: A study of Suicide (1971) by A. Alveraz.

Darkness Visible (2001) by William Styron.

The Bell Jar (1963) by Sylvia Plath.

An Unquiet Mind (1996) by Kay Redfield Jamison.

Bloodletting: A True Story of Secrets, Self-Harm and Survival by Victoria Leatham

The British Medical Journal (BMJ): http://bmj.com

The British Journal of Psychiatry: http://bjp.rcpsych.org/

The American Journal of Psychiatry (AJP): http://ajp.Psychiatryonline.org/

For information I also recommend the World Health Organisation: http://www.who.int/en/

www.ingramcontent.com/pod-product-compliance
Ingram Content Group UK Ltd.
Pitfield, Milton Keynes, MK11 3LW, UK
UKHW041411180426
11947UKWH00007B/69